S0-CIG-213

Trail Markers

Some Thoughts about Getting On and Staying On the Right Trail

Trail Markers

by

Clay T. Buckingham

For family and friends

*"Thy Word is a lamp unto my feet,
and a light unto my path."*
(Psalms 119:105 KJV)

Trail Markers
By Clay T. Buckingham

Copyright © 2018 by Clay T. Buckingham

Scripture references, unless otherwise noted, are taken from the New International Version (NIV). All rights reserved worldwide.

Scriptures noted KJV are from the King James Version of the Bible.

Some scriptures have been paraphrased. Any emphases found in scripture verses are the addition of the author.

Published by Risky Living Ministries, Inc.
www.RLMIN.com

ISBN-13: 978-1720701217

Table of Contents

Introduction 7
#1 It's All About Jesus 11
#2 Memorizing the Word of God 13
#3 Attending Church Regularly 15
#4 Giving 17
#5 Prayer 19
#6 Three Fundamental Decisions 21
#7 Remembering John 3:16 23
#8 Choose Joy 25
#9 Ups and Downs, Twists and Turns 27
#10 Hydrate or Die 29
#11 Enjoy! Take Time for Fun 31
#12 Think Ahead—PLAN 33
#13 Enjoy Your Family! 37
#14 Alcohol 39
#15 Keeping Your Promises 43
#16 The Starting Position 45
#17 What's on Your Mind? 49
#18 Are You on the Right Trail? 51
#19 From Whom Should I Take Advice? 53
#20 Choices 57
#21 How Can I Know? 59
#22 What Are the Constants in Your Life?........ 63
#23 Stay the Course 65
#24 God's Standards for Marriage 67
#25 Lessons from the Book of Ruth 71
#26 Sexuality 75
#27 Reaching Your Destination 77
#28 When a Trail Marker Points in the
       Wrong Direction 81

#29 Decisions 85
#30 My First Trail Marker 89
#31 Trust But Verify 91
#32 In the Beginning (for Me) 93
#33 The Crunch Point 97
#34 Dawn 101
#35 From Darkness to Light 105
#36 The Word of God and the Christian Mind ... 107
#37 Sixty Years on the Marriage Trail 109
#38 The Trail Heads Northwest to Alaska 111
#39 Alaska or Bust 113
#40 Conclusion 117

Introduction

Several years ago, we began a series of periodic email messages to those of our family and friends who are in their teens and twenties and a few in their early thirties. We called them "Trail Markers." We have now consolidated these "Trail Markers" into one publication.

As all hikers know, a trail marker is a small sign, usually nailed to a tree, which marks the trail you want to follow. Often in the wilderness or deep forest, the path becomes indistinct, and there may be many forks in the trail.

It has always been a source of immediate relief and confidence to us when we look along the path and recognize the marker for the trail we want to follow. We know that these markers have been posted by someone who has hiked the trail ahead of us and has placed them along the trail for our benefit.

You are hiking along the "trail of life." We have hiked this trail before you. We have posted these "Trail Markers" for you in the hope that they will provide a useful guide as you also walk this trail.

Our purpose in these messages is to tell you that life is worth living. Or—more pointedly—that living in companionship with Jesus makes life, at every age, worth living.

Also, we want to share with you some of the lessons learned during the 70-plus years that each of us has been a Christian. We want you to know why we, at 90 and 88, can look back over the years with thanksgiving and joy and look forward to the future with confidence and hope.

As we think back over our lives, we can tell you with absolute certainty that with Christ, there is hope and joy. But without Christ, there is nothing left but despair and trouble.

We want to assure you, as we begin, that we have not always been elderly adults. We really were teenagers once, and we have experienced the frustrations, temptations, confusion, doubt, faith, hope, despair and ecstasy which every young person at some time experiences. The vivid experiences of our early years are still burning in our memories—and the old emotions associated with those experiences come flooding back whenever we stop to remember.

We married when we were in our early twenties, raised a family of four children and now are blessed with 21 grandchildren and 27 great-grandchildren.

We have lived in over 25 locations and traveled in 70 countries.

We have experienced both success and failure.

We almost daily experience sin, confession, repentance, forgiveness and restoration.

We have experienced the inexpressible joy of bringing children into the world, but also the deep shock and grief associated with the untimely death of a sibling and the bittersweet sadness coming from the passing of our parents.

We have experienced all of the common negative emotions of anger, perceived rejection, disappointment, uncertainty, doubt, confusion, hardness of heart, guilt, bitterness, anxiety, worry, suspicion and fear, and both of us have known at least some depression.

We have also experienced the positive emotions of joy, hope, peace, happiness, empathy, compassion, confidence, security and love.

Throughout, we have recognized that by building our house—our lives—upon the solid rock of faith in Jesus Christ, we have experienced an underlying stability and sense of well-being. As Isaiah stated in chapter 7, verse 9, "If you do not stand firm in your faith, you will not stand at all."

The mountain of God is there. We see it clearly in good weather. And even when the clouds cover the mountain, we know it is still there, though we cannot see it. And so we have learned to govern our decisions in life based on the confidence that, whether we can see it or not, the mountain is still there.

In retrospect, we realize that we have been held in the palm of His hand all the way. It is His faithfulness and love which have sustained us.

Clay and Clara Buckingham
1076 Grand View Avenue
Everett, Pennsylvania 15537

15 April 2018

Trail Marker #1
It is All About Jesus

"Jesus loves me, this I know..."

Your parents got it right when they taught you this children's song.

One of the great theologians of the last century, when asked to describe the most profound and influential thought of his whole life, stated, "Jesus loves me."

The Gospel of John is the *essence* (the concentrated distillation) of the Christian faith. John 3:16 is the *quintessence* (the essence of the essence, the purest distillation) of the Christian faith: "For God so loved the world that He gave His only son, that whosoever believes in Him should not perish but have everlasting life."

Jesus said, "As the Father hath loved Me, so I have loved you: continue in My love" (John 15:9 KJV).

And, "Greater love hath no man than this, that a man lay down his life for his friends" (John 15:13 KJV).

Throughout our lives, this awareness that "Jesus loves me" has been the most powerful incentive to live the Truth, the most powerful encouragement to keep on in difficult times, and the most powerful deterrent in the face of temptation.

To be loved—personally, intimately, unconditionally—by the Son of the Living God! There is nothing greater in life.

"Jesus loves me." This is the gospel—the Good News.

Make it the continuous and conscious centerpiece of your life.

Trail Marker #2
Christian Disciplines: Memorizing the Word of God

In Trail Marker #1, we talked about the greatest truth of all time: "Jesus loves me."

"Jesus loves me, this I know..."

This children's song goes on to say, "...for the Bible tells me so."

The smartest thing we did when we were young was to memorize Bible verses. Both of us had memorized some Scripture as we were growing up in Sunday school. But shortly after we were married, we began a disciplined program of Bible memorization together.

Although we got diverted from this program as babies began to come, we both consider that this Bible memory program was the most important thing we did to give us a solid foundation for Christian growth and service in future years.

Listening to the preaching of the Word of God, participating in group Bible studies, and personally reading and studying the Bible during daily quiet times—all of this is not only good but also essential for growth as a Christian.

But NOTHING can substitute for MEMORIZING Scripture.

Psalm 1 states, "Blessed is the man...whose delight is in the Law of the Lord, and in His law doth he meditate DAY and NIGHT."

Only by memorizing the Word can you ever hope to meditate on it "day and night." The more Scripture you commit to memory, the more it comes back to mind "day and night" during your everyday living experiences.

We started out using the "Topical Memory System" published by The Navigators. This is still available. Type "Navigators Topical Memory

System" into your search engine and order the first set. It is a small investment which will pay tremendous dividends.

We have talked with many, many young people—ages 15 to 30—who are at loose ends regarding where they are going and what they should be doing with their lives.

The best advice we can give is to use this stage of life to memorize Scripture. God will use it throughout your life in ways which you cannot possibly imagine at this time.

Jesus said, "Man does not live by bread alone, but by every word which proceeds from the mouth of God" (Matthew 4:4).

Just as your physical life depends on a steady intake of food, so your spiritual life depends on a steady intake of the Word of God.

   "I have hidden Your word in my heart [memorized it] that I might not sin against You" (Psalm 119:11).

Start NOW to memorize Scripture.

Trail Marker #3
Christian Disciplines: Attending Church Regularly

"Remember the Sabbath Day, to keep it holy" (Exodus 20:8 KJV).

"[The believers] devoted themselves to biblical teaching, fellowship, communion and prayer" (Acts 2:42).

"Let us not give up meeting together [for worship] as some have done" (Hebrews 10:25).

Fortunately for us, we both grew up in families where regular attendance at Sunday morning worship services was habitual. We continued this habit as we were raising our own family and still make it a practice to attend Sunday morning worship services regardless of where we are.

During the last three decades, as we have traveled more and more, we have met some wonderful new friends and experienced exciting new ways to worship in church services all around the world.

Have you ever heard the excuse, "I don't need to go to church to be a Christian—I can worship God just as well out in the woods"?

This is not what the Bible says. It is nothing but arrogance, pride or ignorance to think that we can live lives pleasing to God without the disciplined, weekly infusion of His Spirit which results from participating in corporate worship.

It is a fact of life that we need one day out of every seven days to be refreshed and rejuvenated both physically and spiritually. Genesis 2:2 records that on the seventh day, God—even God—rested from His work of creation. So who do I think I am—the Energizer Bunny who does not need regular recharging?

Get in the habit—the very good habit—of participating in worship services at a church at least once a week. It is one of the essential disciplines—a trail marker—of the Christian life.

Trail Marker #4
Christian Disciplines: Giving

"For God so LOVED the world that He GAVE..." (John 3:16a KJV).

In Trail Markers #2 and #3, we talked about two of the essential disciplines of the Christian life: memorizing the Word and attending worship services regularly. In this Trail Marker, we will address another of the disciplines of the Christian Life: GIVING.

GIVING is the action word of LOVE: "God so LOVED the world that He GAVE..."

And He gave HIMSELF—in the form of His Son, Jesus Christ.

If we truly LOVE someone, we will very naturally want to GIVE to that person. And the greatest gift we can give is OURSELVES—our time, our attention, our talents and our material resources.

If you truly LOVE Jesus, you will want to GIVE yourself to Him.

The Psalmist said, "The Lord is my shepherd. I shall not WANT." He has given us everything we need. If He is your Shepherd, you will not WANT (long for something more).

Your desire will be to GIVE.

As a matter of fact, you will become a GIVING person, not a GETTING person. Wherever you go, whatever you do, you will have the desire to GIVE, to CONTRIBUTE.

You go to school. You go to work. You go to someone's home. You go to church. Your desire is, "How can I contribute? How can I help? What can I give?"

NOT, "What's in it for ME?"

You meet someone. You think, "How can I encourage this person? How can I enter into this person's life and be helpful?"

NOT, "How can this person help me? How can this person make me happy?"

If you LOVE Jesus, you will want to GIVE to His work here on earth. Give your time, your talents, your money.

Back when we got married, we decided that we would obey God's commandment in Malachi 3:10a: "Bring the whole tithe into the storehouse..." So we started tithing (giving one tenth of) our gross income every month into the Lord's work. The tithe came off of the top of our monthly income— before taxes, before car payments, before food and clothing, before recreation, before toys.

It truly was NOT hard. We simply decided to live off of 90 percent of our income and put the first 10 percent into the Lord's work.

It is a discipline—like memorizing the Word and attending worship services on Sunday.

God goes on to say in Malachi 3:10b, "Test Me in this...and see if I will not throw open the floodgates of heaven and pour out so much blessing that you will not have room enough for it."

As He promised, He blessed our decision to tithe. We have never wanted for sufficient financial resources to meet our everyday needs. And as time went on, and He gave us more and more, we, in turn, were able to give more and more back into His work here on earth.

Are you a GIVING person—or a GETTING person?

Christian Disciplines: Prayer

God IS—God CREATES—God SPEAKS.

He SPOKE the whole universe into existence. And He speaks to us today:

- through His Word

- through His creation

- through history—"His Story"

He also LISTENS.

We contend with a LISTENING God. He HEARS us when we talk to Him. And He is listening even when we refuse to talk with Him.

God came looking for Adam and Eve in the Garden and said, "Adam, where are you?" He expected an answer. An honest, REAL answer!

Of course, God knew exactly where Adam was. But He wanted Adam to know. He wanted Adam to articulate exactly where he "was." Adam needed to know. It was for Adam's own good that God asked that question.

So God comes to you and me, asking, "Where are you?" Where are you REALLY in your walk with Jesus Christ? Where is the REAL you? Where are your REAL interests? Where are your REAL longings? Where are your REAL ambitions? Where are your REAL hopes? Where are your REAL fears? Where is your REAL faith? Where is your mind? Where is your heart?

"Where are you?"

God is asking you these questions. For your own good. YOU need to know where you are.

And God expects REAL answers. He wants you to talk with Him about REAL things—like the condition of your soul.

Is it well with your soul? Or is it not well? Talk to God about it.

Both the Old Testament and New Testament record numerous conversations between men and God. Many of those dialogues don't seem very pious. Some are argumentative. Some are angry. Some are despairing. Some seem to challenge God to "put up or shut up."

But these are REAL conversations. About REAL issues. These REAL men and women were wrestling with REAL answers to God's persistent, penetrating question, "Where are you?"

The disciples asked Jesus, "Teach us to pray." They didn't ask Him to teach them anything else. They saw Jesus praying, and they realized that He received power and solace through His constant communication with God. They wanted to know how to pray like He did.

So Jesus taught them to pray the Lord's Prayer: "Lead us not into temptation, but deliver us from evil." As in REAL temptation. REAL evil.

"Pray without ceasing," the Bible tells us. This doesn't mean we are down on our knees speaking out loud to God in concise, grammatically correct sentences when we are studying calculus, or when we are emptying the garbage. It DOES mean that we are in a constant mental discussion—even debate—with God, always grappling with the REAL answer to God's REAL question, "Where are you?"

REAL prayer is simply discussing REALITY with God.

> *What a friend we have in Jesus,*
> *All our griefs and sins to bear,*
> *What a privilege to carry*
> *Everything to God in prayer.*
> *—Joseph Scriven (1819-1886)*

Trail Marker #6
Three Fundamental Decisions

Many years ago, a wise hiker along the "trail of life" told us that each young person has three basic decisions to make before he or she can be considered fully mature:

1. What do I believe about God?

2. What should I do with my life?

3. Who should be my companion for life?

He also said that these decisions should be made in the order listed above.

The most fundamental question is, "What do I believe about God?" The answer to this question will fundamentally influence the decisions you make regarding the other two questions.

Once you have settled the question about God in your mind and heart, then you have the necessary foundation to move on to the second question, "What should I do with my life?"

Then, once you have made the decision about your life's work and are moving in that direction, you are ready to deal with the third question, "Who should be my companion for life?"

These questions apply to young women as well as to young men—even the question about your life's direction. A girl who spends her twenties and thirties only looking for a husband will miss a whole host of opportunities for joyful service to God and community and may eventually end up frustrated, disappointed and bitter when she finally realizes that God always intended for her to remain single.

Each of these questions requires study, analysis and reflection.

Young people often want to jump ahead to the third question before they have fully answered the first two. But if you haven't really made a decision about God, you have no basis to evaluate the third question.

And if you haven't made a decision about your life's work and started in that direction, you won't be able to enter into a lifetime relationship with another person with confidence and understanding and commitment.

So where are you?

Have you decided what to believe about God? Or are you jumping ahead and wondering about what you should do with your life or whom you should marry before you have settled the fundamental question of faith?

Isaiah stated, "If you do not stand on faith, you will not stand at all."

James stated, "For without faith, it is impossible to please God, for He that comes to God must believe that He is and that He is a rewarder of those who diligently seek Him."

It is the wise young man or young woman who has decided, once and for all, to BELIEVE GOD! And this means to believe what God says in the Bible.

Once this decision is made, you are ready to make the second and then the third decision on your road to real maturity.

Trail Marker #7
Remembering John 3:16

"For God so loved the world that He gave His one and only Son, that whoever believes in Him shall not perish but will have eternal life" (John 3:16).

God loved. Because He loved, He gave. He gave something very precious to Him—His only Son—so that we (you and I), by believing in Him, might receive the most precious gift imaginable: ETERNAL LIFE.

God gave Life. Life abundant. Life everlasting.

God loved. He had compassion on the plight of mankind.

Love is compassion for the condition of others. God knew our condition—sinful, guilty, torn, imprisoned, lost. He sent Jesus to provide for us a way of escape, a way out of our personal wilderness and into His promised land.

The Bible states that Jesus looked out over the crowd and had compassion on them.

Love is taking action—with compassion.

Love is doing—with compassion.

Love is giving—with compassion.

Love is making something good happen in the life of someone else.

God loves you so much that He has made something very good happen in your life. He has given you the assurance that when your body dies, you—THE REAL YOU—will not perish. You will not disappear into oblivion, but rather you will have eternal life in heaven.

Now that is REALLY good news.

In my limited and confined human condition, I cannot give someone else eternal life. But I CAN give something. I can give something which is very precious to me. I can give my TIME. And by so doing, I can make good things happen in other people's lives.

Take TIME for a personal word of encouragement. A phone call. An email. A text message. A word of appreciation to a store clerk or a waitress. A short visit to someone who is lonely. An inexpensive gift. A comforting hug—signifying acceptance, appreciation, affection.

We live in a fallen world. Everyone is hurting. Everyone has fallen short. Everyone wants to be wanted, to be needed, to be loved, to belong, to have friends, to be a part of an accepting, forgiving fellowship.

And everyone has a story.

Ask someone how you can pray for them, and you may catch a glimpse of that secret, turbulent world behind their eyes.

You can make a difference in the life of someone else. You can be Jesus with skin on.

You can make something good happen in someone else's life.

Every day.

Trail Marker #8
Choose Joy

We were climbing up a steep, narrow, rocky path on the Laurel Highlands Trail in Southwestern Pennsylvania. The "Allegheny Outback" participants were dead tired. When we got to the break point overlooking the valley below, the teenagers took off their packs and fell to the ground. Some of them complained out loud about how exhausted they were. Others just lay in the soft grass, trying to catch their breath.

The girls' leader, Tanya Becker, a college student, looked around and made a profound remark to the whole group. As I recall, she said, "There are very few things in life which you can control. But one of the things you CAN control is your attitude. Regardless of the situation or how tired or discouraged you may be, you can choose to be positive, or you can choose to be negative. I urge you to CHOOSE JOY. That is the way out of the wilderness. That is the way of God."

Early in her life, my wife adopted a little saying which has guided her all her life: "Look Up, and Laugh, and Love, and Lift."

Sure, she gets "down" sometimes, usually when she is extremely tired, having spent herself physically and mentally doing something for someone. But she doesn't stay down long.

Her natural proclivity is to:

- LOOK UP to God for encouragement

- Find something funny and LAUGH deeply

- Extend LOVE to those around her

- And LIFT UP those who are REALLY hurting

Whenever you have just about had it with something or someone, that is a good time to "Look Up, and Laugh, and Love, and Lift."

And CHOOSE JOY!

You can do it. It will transform your life and all your relationships with others.

Trail Marker #9
Ups and Downs, Twists and Turns

No trail worth hiking is straight and level the entire distance.

Take, for example, the Cinque Terre, a seven-mile trail which winds up and down along the cliffs of the Mediterranean Coast in northwest Italy, about half way between Pisa and Genoa. We have hiked the Cinque Terre three times, the last time being the summer of 2008 with three grandchildren in tow.

The trail connects five small, picturesque towns perched on the steep mountain slopes above the Mediterranean Sea. It starts at Riomaggiore in the south, at about 200 feet above sea level. It passes through Manarola, Corniglia and Vernazza, and ends in Monterosso, which is down on the water.

Along its course, the trail rises and falls several times, from sea level up to above 800 feet.

In some places it twists and turns through olive groves and grape arbors which hang precariously on the bluffs above the sparkling blue waters of the Mediterranean.

In some areas, where it is relatively level, the trail is five to six feet wide. In other places, where it threads along the cliffs, the trail is less than a foot wide.

In many places along the way, the view is spectacular. In other places, the view is obscured by dense olive groves and other thick foliage.

But even in these obscured areas, we always knew that it wouldn't be long before we would break out into the clear and once again see the beautiful blue Mediterranean Sea, with waves crashing on the rocks far below and sailboats out on the horizon.

It is not an easy trail. But it is worth it. And always, when we would finally get to the end of the trail, down on the beach in Monterosso, we would experience a deep sense of accomplishment, even exhilaration, at having done something hard without giving up.

This is a picture of the trail of life. It is not a straight and level path. There are many severe and seemingly impossibly steep ups and downs, and there are often sudden and confusing twists and turns.

Sometimes it is easy to see the magnificent and breathtaking view of God. But sometimes God is obscured from view by the grind of daily living or the enticement of sin lurking along the trail.

However, in reality, God is always there, and He is always faithful. And for those who do not turn back—who stay the course, who never give up, who keep the faith, who fix their eyes upon Jesus—the rewards, both along the trail and at the end of the trail, are truly awesome.

> *"The desert and the parched land will be glad; the wilderness will rejoice and blossom. Like the crocus, it will burst into bloom; it will rejoice greatly and shout for joy... Water will gush forth in the wilderness, and streams in the desert... A highway [trail] will be there; it will be called the Way [Trail] of Holiness... It will be for those who walk in the Way...only the redeemed will walk on this trail...and at the end of the trail, the redeemed will enter heaven with singing; everlasting joy will crown their heads, gladness and joy will overtake them, and sorrow and sighing will flee away" (Isaiah 35).*

> *"Do not let your hearts be troubled. Trust in God; trust also in Me [Jesus]. In My Father's house are many rooms; if it were not so, I would have told you. I am going there to prepare a place for you. And if I go and prepare a place for you, I will come back to take you with Me that you also may be where I am. You know the way to the place where I am going... I am the way" (John 14).*

Trail Marker #10
Hydrate or Die

We were traveling in Europe with three grandchildren: Stephen (16), Hannah (11) and Katie (8). We had just spent the night in a youth hostel near Interlaken, Switzerland, and were preparing for a day of hiking in the Alps.

Printed in large letters on Hannah's and Katie's water bottles was a statement which warned, "Hydrate or Die."

It was an appropriate warning. Before the day was out, we had hiked about seven miles, the first leg being a 3,000-foot ascent from Lauterbrunnen up to Murren. During the day, we had refilled our water bottles at least five times.

Half way up to Murren, we stopped to rest in a small, green meadow covered with bright yellow flowers. We shared this rest area with several large, brown Swiss cows, each of which had a big copper bell around its neck for location identification.

In the center of the meadow was a long wooden trough filled with clear mountain water, with a drain spout protruding at one end. We decided that this must be for hikers as well as the cows, so we filled our water bottles before continuing our climb up the narrow trail which wound up the steep mountain slope.

Before we reached the top, we had consumed all of the water and refilled our bottles again, this time from a rushing stream which cascaded over big rocks down the mountainside.

Often since then I have thought of that warning on the girls' water bottles: "Hydrate of Die."

The application to our spiritual lives is striking.

We must regularly HYDRATE on the Water of Life or we will shrivel up and die spiritually.

Jesus said, "Whoever drinks the water I give him will never thirst" (John 4:14).

And again, Jesus said, "If a man is thirsty, let him come to Me and drink" (John 7:37).

Every morning, my wife and I read together from the Bible and pray about the activities of the day and for the people we may see. We are HYDRATING.

This morning (Sunday), we attended worship services at the country church down the road. We sang hymns, prayed, heard the Word of God preached, and fellowshipped with other believers. We were HYDRATING.

Do you sometimes feel like a twisted, dried-up sponge, of no use to anyone?

Try HYDRATING regularly on the Word of God.

Trail Marker #11
Enjoy! Take Time for Fun

We were near the end of a three-week trip to Europe with three grandchildren, Stephen, Hannah and Katie. We had spent all day visiting Salzburg ("salt-city"), Austria.

We had walked through museums, castles, parks and cathedrals. We had visited the salt mine, where all of us slid down the long sloping tunnel which links the upper level of the mine to the lower level a hundred or so feet below. We had visited the "Sound of Music" convent where Maria had trained to become a nun.

We had just left Mozart's *geburtshaus* ("house of birth") and the connected museum and were walking to the bus station en route to the youth hostel when we came upon a small *platz* where five streets came together.
In the center of the *platz* was a fountain consisting of about 30 waterspouts shooting up from the broad concrete sidewalk and rising maybe 25 feet in the air.

The weather was warm, and we were all tired and sweaty. We stopped to look at this beautiful and refreshing fountain. We could feel the cooling mist on our faces.

Katie, age 8, turned to me and said, "Grandpa, may I run in the fountain?"

My first reaction was to say, "No, you will get all wet."

And then I thought, what could be more fun for an eight-year-old than to run through a fountain? So I said, "Sure. Have fun."

With a scream of delight, Katie ran into the water and danced about in pure, joyful abandon. The vertical water jets soaked her from every angle.

A group of Japanese tourists turned to watch and take pictures.

And then, out of the corner of my eye, I saw Grandma, ever the school girl at heart, darting toward the fountain.

Hand in hand, grandmother and granddaughter screamed and laughed as they frolicked about in the spewing and cascading cool water.

A crowd had gathered to enjoy the spectacle and cheered and clapped as they witnessed Grandma and Katie, oblivious to their surroundings, immersed in the pure joy of the moment.

As Grandma and Katie returned to where we were standing, Grandma heard the applause of the crowd and immediately felt very self-conscious. Katie, however, was still the epitome of reckless abandon, dancing about in glee. Then she ran into my arms, determined to get me as wet as she was.

Jesus said, "I am come that you might have life, and have it more abundantly."

Certainly, living abundantly includes having fun.

Paul said, "Rejoice in the Lord always, and again I say, rejoice."

REJOICE: To enter again, and again, and again into the delight, bliss and happiness of the life which Jesus has given us so abundantly.

Feel tired, sweaty, worn out, discouraged, burned out?

Find a "fountain" somewhere, take someone with you, and go have some good, clean fun together, enjoying with abandon the life with which God, in His great love, has blessed us beyond measure.

Trail Marker #12
Think ahead – PLAN

Jesus said, "Suppose one of you wants to build a tower. Will he first not sit down and estimate the cost to see if he has enough money to complete it?"

An old proverb states, "If you fail to plan, you are planning to fail."

And failure almost happened.

We were on a two-week trip to the West with our children, Andy (16), Becka (15), Jim (12) and David (5). One of the anticipated events was a hike down to the bottom of the Grand Canyon with the three older children.

Mom and I considered David, at 5, to be a bit young for the long, difficult hike. I promised him that someday I would hike with him to the bottom of the Grand Canyon (the subject of a future Trail Marker.) So Mom and David accompanied us about a half-mile down the trail and then returned back up to our camping place.

I was, I thought, in excellent physical condition. Daily I ran two to three miles and did multiple push-ups and pull-ups.

Also, the three children were in great physical shape.

And they were young.

The difference in elevation from the South Rim of the canyon down the Bright Angel Trail to the Colorado River was 4,400 feet. No problem. Down in the morning. Back up in the afternoon. Piece of cake. I might even jog back up.

We left about 8:30 AM. It was cool, maybe 40 degrees, when we started. We made it down to the Colorado in less than three hours. Our only stop was at Indian Gardens, a shaded rest area about halfway down.

It was sunny the whole way. The further down the canyon we got, the hotter it got.

Down at the river, we rested and played in the silty water. The temperature was now about 95 degrees Fahrenheit.

As we started back up, it was clear to me that this was not going to be as easy as I had thought. Hot. Dusty. Steep. Hiking 4,400 feet up is different than hiking 4,400 feet down.

It was slow-going. Our rate back up was less than half of what it had been going down. I estimated that we should make it back at about 6:30 PM.

At Indian Gardens, we refilled our water bottles and rested for a few minutes.

The steep cliffs of the canyon now blocked out the sun. We were hiking in the shade. The more we ascended, the colder it got.

About 1,000 feet from the crest, I had to stop. The children were OK, although they also were tired. But they were young.

I sent them on ahead and started very slowly up the final ascent, going just a few feet at a time, then resting, then going again.

By the time I got back to the camping area, it was dark. And cold. I literally collapsed. I was extremely fatigued, cold, shivering, and dehydrated.

Although I didn't know it at the time, I was suffering from heat exhaustion.

I curled up in my sleeping bag to try to get warm. I couldn't eat anything or drink anything. Or sleep. My whole body was shaking and cramping. It was a miserable night. Eventually, the next day, I was able to drink a few sips of warm soup.

It took me two full days to recover.

What went wrong?

I was overconfident. I was in good shape for running long distances on flat ground, but not for hiking 4,400 feet down a steep trail and then back up the same day without adequate rest and refreshment.

Nor had I talked with the hiking experts at the park headquarters about conditions we would meet along the trail.

I had failed to plan ahead and "count the cost."

"If you fail to plan, you are planning to fail."

Whatever task you consider, think about it first. Scope it out in your mind. Anticipate what you might encounter. And talk to experts who have already done it.

Your chances of success will then be much, much better.

Trail Marker #13
Enjoy Your Family!

Someone once said that the two most important verses in the Bible are John 3:16 and Zephaniah 3:17.

John 3:16 is familiar: "For God so loved the world..."

Zephaniah 3:17 is not as familiar:

> *"The Lord your God is with you.*
> *He is mighty to save.*
> *He will take great delight in you.*
> *He will quiet you with His love.*
> *He will rejoice over you with singing."*

Five brief but beautiful statements of how God relates to you!

Did you ever consider that God —the Almighty, the Creator of the universe—rejoices over you with singing?

Young fathers, this is how you should relate to your children, exactly as God relates to you:

- You should be WITH them. As often as possible. Physically, intellectually, morally, spiritually. At every stage of their growing-up years.

- You should SAVE them—protect them from every evil influence which would damage them physically, intellectually, morally, spiritually.

- You should TAKE GREAT DELIGHT in them—in every activity of their lives. Really enjoy them. Affirm them. Appreciate them.

- You should QUIET them with YOUR LOVE. When they go through their normal (yes, extreme) ups and downs, you should be their steadying influence. Calm them with your presence and love.

- And you should REJOICE over them with SINGING. Actually sing to them! Whether you have a good voice or not. Take them up in your arms and dance around the room, singing to them. Do it often.

Several years ago, we were having a discussion about Zephaniah 3:17 with a group of fathers at the White Sulphur Springs Conference Center in Manns Choice, Pennsylvania. One father, a tough, serious-minded Coast Guard officer, had a daughter on the teenage kitchen staff.

At the end of the session we broke up and got ready for lunch.

A few minutes later I heard screaming and laughing and scuffling back in the kitchen, where the teenage girls' staff was preparing to bring the food out to the tables. It was bedlam. Certainly, a serious breach of good order and discipline. I rushed in to see what was causing this commotion.

And there was this tall, swarthy Coast Guard officer, with his teenage daughter scooped up in his arms, dancing around the kitchen, singing to her—to the screaming delight of the whole teen staff.

Father, go find your daughter, turn off her cell phone, take her up in your arms and sing to her.

Daughter, go find your father, turn off his computer, jump into his arms and tell him to sing to you.

Enjoy your family!

Trail Marker #14
Alcohol

Although the Bible does not prohibit drinking wine in moderation, it does get very explicit in warning of the dire consequences of drinking too much. The Bible also describes in graphic detail the effect alcohol has on your mind and body, and specifically on your conduct.

There are indications that when Jesus had a meal at someone's house, He drank the wine offered to Him. It was alcoholic wine. Maybe not as strong as the wine of today, but alcoholic just the same.

Listen to these verses from Proverbs:

> *"Do not join those who drink too much wine... Who has woe? Who has sorrow? Who has strife? Who has complaints? Who has needless bruises? Who has bloodshot eyes? Those who linger over wine... In the end it bites like a snake, and poisons like a viper. Your eyes will see strange sights and your mind will imagine confusing things" (Proverbs 23:20, 29-30, 32-33).*

Alcohol is an addictive drug, like cocaine and nicotine. Some people are much more prone to alcohol addiction than others. But there is no way of knowing in advance. However, you *can* know for certain that you will never become an alcoholic if you never take the first drink.

Alcohol is a depressant. It is a mind-altering drug. It anesthetizes the nerve endings in the brain and thus dulls perception, judgment, awareness and sensitivity.

The first effect of drinking alcohol is the weakening of moral resolve. The person may still know what is right and wrong, but the commitment to do right and avoid wrong, and the awareness of long term consequences, begins to fade after a couple of beers or a glass of wine. Under the progressive, imperceptible, deceptive influence of alcohol, a person's attitude toward right and wrong conduct gradually becomes one of, "What does it matter? Who cares? It's not all that bad. Let's do it."

This is especially true in the realm of sexual temptation.

The following story is a fictionalized composite of several true situations we know about.

A 19-year-old girl, a sophomore at a state university, attends a Christian student leadership meeting at the off-campus apartment of the student leader, a senior, a young man whom she admires and secretly likes. During the meeting, she catches his eye several times and, once, when he smiles at her, she feels a thrill of excitement.

As the meeting ends, he asks her to stay for a few minutes to listen to some Christian music he has recently purchased. He will drive her to her dorm afterward, he promises.

When everyone else has departed, he puts on the music and then gets a bottle of wine from his closet. He pours himself a glass and casually offers one to the girl. Although she has never tasted an alcoholic beverage before and is inwardly reluctant, she accepts the wine because he is such a respected campus leader, and she certainly does not want to come across to him as prudish or legalistic.

The wine is sweet and exciting. They sit on the couch together, slowly drinking the wine, talking of campus ministry, and listening to the soft, soothing music.

As the time passes, their "fellowship" becomes increasingly warm and intimate. One glass calls for another. She finds the wine so smooth, so easy and pleasant to drink.

Within an hour, after two glasses of wine, the relaxing effect of the alcohol has released her from all anxiety, and the world has become a beautiful and friendly place, full of new and pleasant feelings. She is entirely at ease now, comfortable, accepted, at peace. His strong arm, draped around her shoulders, is warm and exciting and reassuring. She lays her head back on his shoulder.

Another half hour slips by as she slowly finishes her third glass of wine. Her head is swimming. Although she does not realize it, her deeply-rooted

Christian inhibitions—those powerful tethers of conscience which restrain a person from willful sin—have loosened and dissolved, allowing her natural sexual instincts slowly and imperceptibly to take control of her mind and body.

Deep in her heart, she knows exactly where this is leading and that it is sinful before God; but in her semi-conscious, wine-saturated state of mind, she doesn't care. She is willing now, even eager, to go there.

And what does it matter? It doesn't. Because she is lost in the woods, floating down a gentle stream through a fragrant meadow, untethered and free, consumed by the new and exciting sexual sensations which are propelling her onward and onward and onward; she is another person, in another world, far away, where nothing matters and everything is beautiful and scented and wonderful and timeless and romantic and acceptable, and God is nowhere.

Waking up slowly the next morning in her own room, she struggles to remember the details of the night before. Where was she? Why was she there? How did she get home?

One specific memory slowly begins to emerge in her mind and dominate her consciousness. She remembers, now, that in the process of the wine working its malicious magic on her mind and body, she had willingly submitted to the young man's gentle and progressive advances; and, without any sense of wrong-doing, had easily surrendered her virginity to him.

She realizes now that it was the mesmerizing influence of the wine that had made it all seem so smooth, so natural, so compelling, so exciting, so good, so right, so pure.

Becoming fully awake and conscious of her situation and surroundings, she now feels dirty, degraded, deceived, mocked, her privacy invaded, her inner person compromised.

Suddenly she hates everything about that evening. She hates him. She hates his apartment. She hates his music. She hates his cologne. She hates his calm, coaxing, persuasive voice. She hates his wine. The mental image of that dark, mysterious bottle makes her physically sick. And she hates his Bible, which had lain open all evening on the table in front of the couch, right beside the bottle of wine.

But most of all, she hates herself for accepting that first glass of wine. A sour, throbbing, consuming sense of guilt and remorse begins to flood into her soul. And fear—soul-wrenching, scorching, terrible fear. The word will get out. Boys like to brag. Girls like to gossip. Her family will find out. She will be disgraced. How can she ever again face her parents, her brothers, her Christian friends?

She is ruined. She is trapped. Maybe she is pregnant. She wants to scream, to run, to escape, to hide, to disappear, even to die.

Here is the end of the matter:

"Wine is a mocker and strong drink is raging, and whosoever is deceived thereby is not wise" (Proverbs 20:1 KJV).

Trail Marker #15
Keeping Your Promises

The first time we hiked down to the bottom of the Grand Canyon, I took Andy, Becka and Jim, our three oldest children. David, our youngest, was 5 at the time. He was just too young to go, so he and Mom stayed back.

Before we started down, I promised David I would do the hike with him someday when he was older.

About 14 years later, when David was 19 and had just completed his first year at Penn State, Clara and I took him on a five-week trip out West. We drove all the way from Pennsylvania to California, stopping at national and state parks to camp, hike and enjoy God's wonderful world.

Grand Canyon National Park was a prime stop on our trip.

This time, David and I hiked down the South Kaibab Trail (4,780 feet top to bottom) in the afternoon, camped that night at the Bright Angel Campground at the bottom of the canyon, and hiked back up the Bright Angel Trail the next morning.

Except for fending off the mule deer that were numerous down at the camp site and very persistent in trying to get to our food, the hike down and back was without serious incident.

David and I had a great father-son time together on that hike. However, the most important thing about it was that I had kept my 14-year-old promise to hike down to the bottom of the Grand Canyon with him.

Back in my mid-teens, when I was doing a lot of hiking and camping with the Boy Scouts, I memorized Robert Service's classic poem, "The Cremation of Sam McGee," a harrowing tale of the Gold Rush days in the Yukon Territory of Northwest Canada.

One verse still registers brightly in my mind:

Now a promise made is a debt unpaid
And the trail has its own stern code.

I had made a promise to David. It was a debt unpaid. I paid that debt when we made that hike down and back 14 years after I had made the promise and incurred the debt.

Back when I was a second-year student at West Point, I made a promise to follow Jesus. For the rest of my life. No turning back.

It is a debt I voluntarily incurred which I am still paying off.

It was a promise I made based on HIS promise to me to give me a life worth living and eternal life with Him if I would follow Him—just one of His many "great and precious promises" (2 Peter 1:4 KJV).

When I became an officer in the U.S. Army, I made a promise "to support and defend the Constitution of the United States of America against all enemies, foreign and domestic..."

It is a debt I voluntarily incurred which I am still paying off.

Three years later I made a promise to Clara as we stood at the altar, to love and respect and honor her as my wife, for better or for worse, in sickness or in health, forsaking all others, till death do us part.

It is a debt I voluntarily incurred which I am still joyfully paying off.

Can people trust you to keep your promises? When you say you will do something, do you actually do it?

When you make a promise, do you consider it a "debt unpaid"?

God does.

HE keeps HIS promises.

Do you keep yours?

Trail Marker #16
The Starting Position

Many years ago, when I was a battalion commander, I would regularly lead the battalion in group calisthenics.

From my position on a five-foot platform, with about 600 soldiers in a square formation in front of me, I would start the grueling 30-minute procedure by announcing the first exercise—for instance, the two-count pushup.

Then I would command, "Starting position, MOVE." The soldiers would immediately drop into the "front leaning rest" position, ready to begin the exercise.

Next I would command, "Ready, EXERCISE." Then we would begin doing pushups, shouting as we exercised, "One-two-three-ONE; one-two-three-TWO; one-two-three-THREE; one-two-three-FOUR," and on up until we had all done maybe 40 or 50 pushups.

Then I would command, "Position of attention, MOVE," and everyone would spring to their feet in a position of attention, prepared to begin the next exercise.

It was a great routine, designed to produce strong, healthy, physically fit bodies, capable of withstanding the physical rigors of combat.

But suppose no one got beyond the starting position and simply remained in the "front leaning rest" position for the entire period? Obviously, the whole purpose of doing calisthenics would be negated, and no one would get any physical benefit from the procedure.

This is like the Christian life. Many people never get past the starting position. They make a profession of faith; they accept Jesus Christ as their Lord and Savior; they are saved, born again, regenerated, converted, or whatever you want to call it.

And it is certainly true that no one can live the Christian life unless he or she has first taken the starting position.

But this is just the beginning. Sadly, many go through life never having advanced much beyond the starting position. They profess salvation. They know the salvation language. They enjoy the music. They are warmed by the fellowship.

However, their lives show no fruit. They don't know the Bible. They are not disciplined by the Scripture.

They are still in the starting position.

God wants us to grow into maturity as Christians. His purpose is to produce men and women who are "conformed to the image" of Jesus Christ—who are like Jesus Christ in their character and their outlook on life. Men and women:

- who are fair, compassionate, faithful, forgiving, tough, resilient, giving, serving.

- who look out for the poor, the disadvantaged, the weak, the sick, the orphaned, the widowed, the grieving, the lonely, the discouraged.

- who will "feed His sheep" with the teaching of the Word of God.

- who will never give up or turn back, even if it means suffering and possibly death.

The Christian faith is a two-part process. First is accepting Jesus Christ as Lord and Savior. Second is growing to maturity in Christ.

The Bible compares the Christian life to physical life. We are born, and then we grow into maturity. But physical growth requires both food and exercise. So does spiritual growth.

For the Christian, our spiritual food is the Word of God.

And for the Christian, our exercise is obeying the commandments of God as found in the Bible.

The Bible teaches that each must first assume the starting position (faith) but then rapidly progress into the exercise routine (obedience).

James says that "faith without works is dead." Assuming the starting position (faith) but never exercising (works) is useless.

Take an honest look at yourself. Are you doing the calisthenics—growing into the likeness of Jesus Christ by taking in the Word of God and obeying His commandments?

Or are you still lingering in the starting position?

Trail Marker #17
What's on Your Mind?

Recently, a friend asked me casually, "What's on your mind?"

His question got me to thinking.

What IS on my mind?

What ARE the things which are CONSTANTLY on my mind?

What thoughts constitute the MENTAL BACKDROP of my life?

Here they are:

- That God IS, that He creates, that He speaks, that He listens, and that He loves me.

- That Jesus Christ lives in my heart by the Holy Spirit.

- That I hear His voice through Scripture and conscience.

- That I am married to my wonderful Clara, who is my friend, my companion, my helper, my lover, the constant "wind under my wings."

- That I am blessed beyond measure by family—children, grandchildren, great-grandchildren, brothers, sisters, cousins, nieces, nephews.

- That my friends in Christ—who are of all ages and live all around the world—are a constant inspiration and source of fulfillment to me.

- That I am a man, a husband, a father, a grandfather, a great-grandfather, a neighbor, an American citizen, a soldier—and that each of these roles carries distinct and continuous responsibilities.

- That in each of these roles, my personal calling from God, as a follower of Jesus Christ, is to take up my "cross," to shoulder my responsibilities, and follow Him—joyfully.

- That God's Word is living and powerful, discerning the thoughts and intents of my heart.

- That I cannot be at peace with my wife, my family, my friends and the world around me unless I am at peace with myself, and that I cannot be at peace with myself unless I am at peace with God.

- That I sin in thought, word and deed, and that only through recognition of that sin, sincere confession and repentance can I be at peace with God, and therefore at peace with myself, and therefore at peace with wife, my family, my friends and the world around me.

- That there are no permanent successes or failures.

- That the world is full of both good and evil.

- That life is full of both joy and sadness.

- That God is faithful. I can take Him at His word. He gives strength for today and hope for tomorrow.

- That I have a reserved place in Heaven, established there personally for me by Jesus Christ Himself.

So, "What's on my mind?" These things—constantly.

Trail Marker #18
Are You on the Right Trail?

Are you on the right trail? It DOES make a difference.

The right trail begins with Genesis 1.

> *"In the beginning, GOD..."*

This is the fundamental cornerstone of faith. If I understand and firmly hold that GOD was IN THE BEGINNING, then the whole of the Christian faith ultimately makes sense, and life has purpose. If I do not, then life has no purpose and I am lost, thrashing about in meaningless intellectual and moral chaos, without direction, meaning or anchor.

> "In the beginning, GOD CREATED..."

There is no other reasonable explanation. How was endless time created? How was endless space created? How was all life created?

Evolutionists can go back in logic just so far, but they cannot explain from their theory how LIFE started. To suggest that LIFE created itself, that it simply came into being, that it evolved out of some primordial quagmire, is nothing more than a senseless, wild guess. To believe the Scripture, that *"GOD CREATED,"* makes ultimate sense and gives us a solid rock on which to stand.

And what about me? Who created me? Who made me "me" and not someone else? How did *the essential me* (my awareness, my comprehension, my understanding, my emotions, my ability to think and reason, my memory, my spirit and soul) get lodged in this particular physical body, at this point in time, in this culture, in this place?

My body will die and return to dust. That is for sure. But how about *the essential me*? To believe that God placed *the essential me* in THIS body at THIS point in time, in THIS culture and in THIS place, and that He has prepared a home for *the essential me* in an endless heaven, as Jesus promises, is the foundation for JOY, PEACE, CONFIDENCE, PURPOSE AND LIFE. Any alternative belief will ultimately result in confusion, despondency, despair, and death.

There are many things about your life that you cannot control. But you CAN choose what you will believe. You CAN choose your trail. And in the long run, that is the most important and enduring choice you can ever make.

That is, if you want to get to where you hope you are going.

"Therefore CHOOSE LIFE..." (Deuteronomy 30:19 KJV)

This is the right trail.

All other trails lead to oblivion.

Trail Marker #19
From Whom Should I take Advice?

We had just landed at Heathrow, the giant international airport just outside of London. We went through immigration and customs, collected our bags, rented a car and were ready to head to Bath, a city about 100 miles west-southwest of London. This meant finding our way out of the airport complex and onto Motorway M4, the British equivalent of an American interstate highway.

Getting out of Heathrow is like finding the correct end of the correct piece of spaghetti and following it as it twists and turns through the whole massive spaghetti bowl.

We had just gotten seated in our rental car. As driver, I was trying to get accustomed to sitting on the right-hand side and operating the gear shift lever with my left hand.

I also knew that within moments I would be faced with an even more intimidating situation: driving on the left-hand side of the road in heavy, merciless, fast, unforgiving traffic.

What all this meant was that I had to start thinking into a mirror, with everything reversed.

Before starting the car, I asked the rental car lot attendant how to find my way to M4 once I was out of the parking lot.

He emphasized that I should turn LEFT immediately after going through the rental car exit gate and gave very clear directions on what to do after leaving the gate: "Take two immediate right turns, go to the second traffic light, turn left, go about 100 yards, turn left again, go one-half mile to a stop sign, turn right and then follow the blue signs marked 'Toward M4.'"

As we approached the exit gate, I decided to confirm these directions by asking the guard standing in the booth at the gate. The guard stated emphatically that I needed to turn RIGHT as I exited the gate. He took my papers and waved me through the gate.

I paused and questioned the guard on this, explaining that the parking lot man had said turn LEFT upon exiting the gate. But the guard was adamant that I should turn RIGHT.

With the option of turning LEFT or turning RIGHT immediately ahead, I looked again at the parking lot map and got out my compass to orient myself.

It seemed very clear to me that I should follow the first advice and turn LEFT.

By this time cars were lining up behind us, and the guard was waving his arms and pointing me toward the RIGHT-hand turn.

I hesitated again, but horns started blowing and the guard began shouting things which were not very complimentary of my mental faculties.

Maybe he is right, I thought. Maybe I had misunderstood the first giver of directions. Maybe in my haste I had the map upside down. Or maybe my compass was as confused as I was.

So I moved ahead and turned RIGHT.

As we exited the parking lot, I began to follow the directions as given by the original information-giver: "Take two immediate right turns, go to the second traffic light, turn left, go about 100 yards, turn left again, go one-half mile..."

At first we seemed to be doing OK. But soon things began to go sour.

Within minutes, we were on a one-lane dirt road with no other cars in sight, and there were no blue signs marked "Toward M4."

We turned around when the road petered out near a very high chain-link fence at the end of one of the runways.

What went wrong?

Simply stated, I followed bad advice.

The first man was right, confirmed by my map and compass. But under the pressure of the moment and the influence of the guard, I chose to follow bad advice.

Someone who seemed to know and who was very convincing—almost demanding—gave me bad advice, and I took it.

When considering the way to go, from whom should I take advice?

The guard gave me advice which was contrary to my map and compass. I should have relied on my map and compass.

The Bible says:

> *"Your statutes are my delight; they are my counselors" (Psalm 119:24).*

> *"Your Word is a lamp for my feet, a light on my path" (Psalm 119:105).*

On questions of right and wrong, I should always be guided by the Word of God, which is the map and compass for my life. God's Word is the only advisor that ALWAYS gives good advice.

Anyone who gives advice which is inconsistent with the Word of God is giving bad advice.

Trust and follow your map and compass: the Bible, the Word of God.

Always.

Trail Marker #20
Choices

We were with a group of people and had a free day in a beautiful European city. Most of the group chose to spend the day visiting shops, cafes and theaters. A small group chose to climb up a long, rocky, winding trail which ascended through a thick forest to an ancient monastery situated on a mountain overlooking the city. There they got a magnificent view of not only the great city but also the entire landscape—and watched in awe as God unveiled one of His most beautiful sunsets.

Life is all about choices.

In Interlaken, Switzerland, with three grandchildren, we had two days for hiking in the Alps. There were many trails to choose from. Some were steep mountain paths which led up toward snow-covered peaks with many spectacular views of waterfalls and green valleys far below. Other trails, less demanding, generally wound through lush valleys and meadows. We chose to head for the heights. We were not disappointed.

How should you make decisions on which trails to take?

In Deuteronomy, Moses, speaking the words of God, exclaimed:

> *"This day...I have set before you life and death, blessings and curses. Now choose life, so that you and your children may live and that you may love the Lord your God, listen to His voice and hold fast to Him. For the Lord is your life"* (Deuteronomy 30:19-20).

The moment you choose to live your life completely surrendered to Jesus Christ, you choose to follow the trail that leads to LIFE. At that moment, the Holy Spirit—the third Person of the Trinity (God the Father, God the Son, and God the Holy Spirit)—enters into you to be your ever-present Teacher, Enabler, and Trail Guide.

As a Christian, throughout your whole life, whatever you spend your life doing, you will be faced with moral decisions. You will be faced with choosing either the harder right or the easier wrong. You should make these decisions with your intellect informed and guided by the Holy Spirit within you.

Do you want to know what God's will is for your life?

God does not have a specific plan for your life. He leaves the choice up to you.

But He does have a specific purpose. And here is His purpose for your life, taken from 2 Peter 1:3-8:

> *"As we get to know Jesus better, His divine power (the Holy Spirit living within us) gives us everything we need for living a godly life. He has called us to receive His own glory and goodness. And by that same mighty power, He has given us all of His rich and wonderful promises. He has promised that you will escape the decadence all around you caused by evil desires and that you will share in His divine nature. For this very reason, make every effort to add moral excellence to your faith; and to moral excellence, add wisdom and understanding; and to wisdom and understanding, add self-control; and to self-control, add perseverance; and to perseverance, add a Christ-like attitude; and to a Christ-like attitude, add love for other Christians; and finally you will grow to have genuine love for everyone. The more you grow in love like this, the more you will become productive and useful in your knowledge of our Lord Jesus Christ."*

This is God's purpose for your life—regardless of what you choose for your college or occupation, or who you choose for your spouse.

> *"May the God of hope fill you with all joy and peace as you trust in Him, so that you may overflow with hope, by the power of the Holy Spirit"* (Romans 15:13).

How Can I Know?

We recently had two young women ask essentially the same question: How can I know if a person is the one with whom I want to spend the rest of my life?"

One put it this way: "Do you think that God specifically calls people to marriage?"

Our response: "YES."

"If so, what does this *call to marriage* look like?"

Our response: "It is an overwhelming SPIRITUAL and PHYSICAL attraction between a man and a woman who BOTH are certain that their desires and eligibility for marriage are fully consistent with God's standards for marriage."

"How does God reveal that to you? For instance, you are dating someone, and you know that the person you are dating is someone you could marry, but you aren't sure whether this is God's will for you. How can you know?"

Our response: "If you both personally have prayed deeply and comprehensively about your relationship with each other and have discussed your expectations for marriage fully with each other, and you both CONTINUE to experience that overwhelming SPIRITUAL and PHYSICAL attraction, then you should marry."

With both young women, we continued our counsel with guidelines for evaluating a relationship, in order to answer the question, "How can I know?"

You can never know *without any doubt*. It is always a leap of faith. But there are many valuable practical indicators:

- "Do not be yoked together with an unbeliever..." (2 Corinthians 6:14). It is a fundamental biblical rule that a Christian should not marry a non-Christian. A believing woman who marries an unbelieving man will NEVER be truly "at one" with her husband. That is because HER life is hidden with Christ in God and HIS life is not. It simply never works well.

- Is he attractive to you? Not just in a sexual way, but do you respect and admire him?

- Do you enjoy his company? Do you enjoy being with him? Does being with him make you feel better about yourself?

- When you are with him, do you feel encouraged and strengthened, uplifted, more spiritually motivated?

- Does the thought of seeing him on a weekend make your heart skip a beat, make you sing to yourself, enjoy what you are doing?

So, up front:

- Is he a man of faith—a believer who has entered into a personal relationship with God through Jesus Christ, who recognizes that God loves him and has a purpose for his life?

- Does he have a strong conscience—meaning, can he tell right from wrong, and does he know that God holds him accountable for his thoughts, words, deeds?

- How important is his Christian faith in his life?

Then there are also other things:

- Is he a positive person or a negative person? Does he see good in life and in people? Or does he, most of the time, see bad in life and in people? Is he positive or negative about his parents?

- Does he face difficulties with a good spirit? Is he a laughing, cheerful person? Does he "Look up, and laugh, and love, and lift"?

- Does he like people? Does he meet people easily? Does he have a lot of friends? Have you met any of them? Do you like them? Are you comfortable with them? How does he relate to them?

- Is he a spiritual leader? Are you willing and eager for him to be YOUR spiritual leader?

- How does he treat you? Is he gentle? Courteous? Tender? Generous? Giving?

- Is he courteous to others? Do you know any members of his family? How does he treat them?

- Is he honest? Can you trust him? Does he keep his promises? Is he reliable? Can you depend on him?

- Is he a go-getter? A leader? Aggressive in his work? Does he take responsibility for his actions?

- Does he want you to be his WIFE and lifetime COMPANION? Or does he want you to be his "mother," his provider, his nurse, his caretaker?

- Does he truly like being with you? Is he truly interested in the real spiritual and intellectual you? Or is it your body he lusts after? If he wants sex before you are married, dump him now! If you give him sex now, he won't ever want to get married. As one guy said, "Why buy the cow if you can get the milk free?"

- Is he educated? A thinker? Does he keep up with the world?

- What does he like to do in his spare time? Is he an outside man who loves the woods, the lakes, the trees? Is he an inside man who reads, studies, thinks, plans? Or don't you know? Does he spend his spare time just watching TV and movies or playing video games?

- What does he think about a man's role in the home? Will he be the leader? Will he share the household responsibilities? Or does he expect you to do all the household chores—like cleaning, dish washing—while he is amusing himself in front of the TV?

And now back to YOU:

- Would you like to spend the rest of your life with him, even if you can't have children? Can you see him as a lifelong friend, companion, partner?

- Are you willing for him to be your leader, to make the big decisions in your life and in your family? Would you be willing to subordinate your own desires and career in order to enhance his career? You must marry someone stronger spiritually than you are and to whom you will willingly submit if you are to be truly happy.

- Would you like him to be the father of your children? To be the one who leads not only you but your children—your whole family? Is he capable of doing this? Is he ALREADY leading you spiritually?

And after thinking all of this through:

- Would you like to sleep in the same bed with him, every night, for the rest of your life?

Finally, your HEART must be in it:

- Are you really in love with him? Do you feel like you can't live without him?

Think on all of these things before you make up your mind.

Trail Marker #22
What are the Constants in Your Life?

It was almost dark. I was walking alone on a hillside trail about 500 feet above a little village in northern Italy. I was heading back down to the warmth and peace and merriment of the home where our son, his wife and five children, and my wife were preparing for the evening meal.

It was overcast, and lights in the village below created a soft, muted, rosy glow in the mist which was descending over the valley.

I stopped to enjoy the sheer beauty of the scene.

I imagined the lights to represent the constants which have filled my mind and heart and caused a peaceful, joyful and hopeful glow to light up most of my life. I began to identify and catalogue those constants. Here are the most compelling:

- I have an abiding awareness of God—that He exists, that He created me, that He loves me. My parents were believers in God, and I absorbed from them a belief in the fact of God.

- More than just a believer in God, I am also a Christian. It was in college that I seriously decided to *follow Jesus*, which I gradually came to recognize as being born again, saved, regenerated, converted.

- The Word of God has deeply influenced my thinking and actions. I resonate to Hebrews 4:12: "For the Word of God is quick and powerful, and sharper than any two-edged sword, piercing even to the dividing asunder of soul and spirit, and of the joints and marrow, and is a discerner of the thoughts and intents of the heart" (KJV).

- God has a purpose for my life, and that purpose is to grow into the likeness (character) of Jesus Christ.

- I am not the center of this world, nor am I alone in this world; Jesus Christ is the center, and I am a member of the family of God, the corporate body of Christ, the worldwide church of the Living God.

- The true mark of a Christian is to "…do justly, and to love mercy, and to walk humbly with thy God" (Micah 6:8 KJV).

- I am constantly torn between what I know through Scripture to be good and evil and the dark side of my nature, which beckons me to turn back and surrender to "the lust of the flesh, and the lust of the eyes, and the pride of life" (1 John 2:16 KJV).

- By God's grace, He gave me Clara, who has for more than 65 years been my constant companion, my best friend, my most trusted advisor, my greatest encourager, and my faithful and only lover.

- I am a husband, a father, a grandfather and now a great-grandfather, and each of these roles carries with it responsibilities which can be fulfilled by no one but me.

- I am an American soldier—retired, yes, but still carrying in my knapsack the mark of the military profession; and the oath of office I took over 70 years ago—to support and defend the Constitution of the United States against all enemies, both foreign and domestic—has never been revoked.

- I live in a country and in a world which, at one and the same time, is both good and evil; and there exists, side by side, both love and hate, beauty and ugliness, joy and sadness, peace and strife, those who believe and those who do not.

- When I die, I have a reserved place in Heaven in the company of my Lord and Savior Jesus Christ (John 14:1-3).

These are some of the constants which day and night fill my mind and heart. They are the steady lights of a "heavenly village" which cast a comforting, hopeful and beautiful glow on the descending mists of old age.

Trail Marker #23
Stay the Course

"Ponder the path of thy feet and let thy ways be established" (Proverbs 4:26 KJV).

During the past week, we have been in consultation with three different individuals, each of whom is facing a major decision. Each situation is different. But in each case, whatever decision is made will surely change the life of that person permanently.

One involves a young man who is considering giving up a valuable scholarship and dropping out of college.

One involves a young woman in her mid-twenties who is considering breaking off her engagement to be married.

One involves a highly respected, retired professional, now in public Christian ministry, who has been openly but unjustly accused of wrongdoing by co-workers.

Proverbs teaches us that we should PONDER the path we are about to take. This means consider and evaluate, in the light of God's love and grace, every ramification of the decision, both pro and con.

And we should follow only a FIRM path. This means a path which has a solid, unshakable, godly foundation and leads toward a godly destination.

Throughout our lives we are all faced with decisions. Learning to make godly decisions is a crucial part of growing as a Christian.

We are always in some way or another approaching a place where there is a path leading away from the path we are currently on. Jesus warned about putting our shoulder to the plow and then looking back. Unless the path we are now on has no firm foundation and is obviously leading either nowhere or toward some evil destination, we should stay on the path we are on.

Trail Marker #24
God's Standards for Marriage

Are you a single man or woman who would like someday to be married?

Are you married, but have never really studied the biblical standards for marriage?

Here are some scripture passages to think about, along with our comments.

<u>For the (future) wife</u>:

> Genesis 2:18: *"The Lord God said, 'It is not good for a man to be alone. I will make a helper suitable for him."*

The principal role of a wife is to BE THERE for her husband so that he will not be alone. She is a complement for him. She completes him. But she must BE THERE for him in order to do this. She must BE THERE physically, intellectually, emotionally, spiritually and sexually. She should think about each of these aspects of BEING THERE so that he will *never* feel alone in any of them. She is to be his companion, friend, lover. A successful marriage depends on the wife BEING THERE for her husband.

And she is to HELP him. This doesn't mean boss him or run his life. But it does mean that wherever and whenever she can, she is to HELP him. This could mean making sure he has clean underwear and socks and pressed clothing to wear each day; making sure that he has a good breakfast before going to work; encouraging him when he is stressed out; making sure that he gets enough sleep; taking care of administrative things, such as letter writing, phone calls, housekeeping, laundry and grocery shopping; and doing everything possible to make his professional job easier for him to handle.

> Song of Solomon 2:3: *"Like an apple tree among the trees of the forest is my beloved among the young men. I delight to sit in his shade and his fruit is sweet to my taste."*

In God's plan for the family, the wife voluntarily subordinates herself to her husband. She is to consider him always the "apple of her eye" and always treat him like he is the best of the bunch.

When Scripture says she "delights to sit in HIS shade, and HIS fruit is sweet to [her] taste," it means that the wife rejoices in her husband's successes. They are *her* successes. She does not need to go out and make a career for herself in order to get her kicks. She is now a part of her husband and she revels in HIS enjoyment of HIS work. She goes where he goes, eagerly, not reluctantly. She is his cheerleader.

Above all else, a husband wants his wife to BE THERE for him, supporting him, helping him in every aspect of his life.

For the (future) husband:

> Proverbs 5:15-17: *"Drink water from your own cistern, running water from your own well. Should your springs overflow in the streets, your streams in the public square? Let them be yours alone, never to be shared with strangers."*

Proverbs was written by Solomon, the same man who wrote the Song of Solomon. In these verses, Solomon is saying that a man is to be faithful to his wife—all of his life:

- *"Drink water from your OWN cistern, running water from your OWN well."* Fulfill your sexual need with your wife only.

- *"Should your SPRINGS overflow in the streets, your STREAMS in the public square? Let them be yours alone, never to be shared with strangers."* Springs and streams are a reference to a man's sperm-laden semen. It should never be shared with anyone but his wife.

- *"May your FOUNTAIN be blessed."* Another reference to a man's semen. May it cause him to have many children.

- *"May your fountain be blessed and may you rejoice in the wife of your youth. A loving doe, a graceful deer—may her breasts satisfy you always, may you ever be captivated by her love"* (Proverbs 5:18-19). Pretty self-explanatory. Your wife is to be your one and only lover, as long as you both shall live.

For both husband and wife:

Genesis 1:27: *"So God created mankind in His own image...male and female He created them."*

God created man and woman EQUAL in His sight. Both are to love and respect the other. Neither is to try to dominate the other. In the sight of God, they are equal.

Ephesians 5:22-25: *"Wives, submit to your own husbands as you do to the Lord. For the husband is the head of the wife as Christ is the head of the church, His body, of which He is the Savior. Now as the church submits to Christ, so also wives should submit to their husbands in everything. Husbands, love your wives just as Christ loved the church and gave Himself up for her."*

In the marriage relationship, in order for it to prosper, God places the man in authority over his wife, but this does not lessen her value or equality. The husband's duty is to love, protect and provide for his wife, just as Christ did for the church. His wife's duty is to be there for her husband, to help him, to encourage him and to obey him.

The wife is to be subject to her husband in all things. However, there are two important exceptions:

- If the husband commands his wife to do something which God forbids, she is not required to do it.

- If the husband forbids his wife from doing something God commands, the wife may go on and do it.

For both the husband and the wife there is a higher loyalty, and that is to God.

Decide now that you will read Scripture together and pray together EVERY DAY. You can do this early in the morning or at night. But the essential thing is to covenant with God and each other to do this. It is the key to staying close together personally and close to the Lord.

Lessons from the Book of Ruth

For both men and women: Making the Right Choice

> *Ruth 1:16-17: "But Ruth replied [to Naomi, her widowed mother in law], 'Don't urge me to leave you or turn back from you. Where you go I will go, and where you stay I will stay. Your people will be my people and your God my God. Where you die I will die, and there I will be buried...'"*

Ruth, in her twenties, childless and recently widowed, had a choice to make: either return to her homeland and look for another husband, or stay with her mother-in-law and be her lifelong companion. Ruth chose the latter: service above self. This is always the right choice.

For both men and women: Service as a Sacrifice to God

> *Ruth 2:2,7: "And Ruth...said to Naomi, 'Let me go to the fields and pick up the leftover grain...' Naomi said to her, 'Go ahead my daughter... She came into the field and has remained here from morning till now, except for a short rest in the shelter.'"*

Service is hard work. It is not accompanied by background music or commercial breaks or crowd applause. The only reward for service is the sure knowledge that it is the right thing to do.

For men: Godly Leadership

> *Ruth 2:4-5: "Boaz [who owned the field] arrived from Bethlehem and greeted the harvesters, 'The Lord be with you.' 'The Lord bless you,' they answered. Boaz asked the overseers of his harvesters, 'Who does that young woman belong to?' The overseer replied, 'She is the Moabite who came back from Moab with Naomi.'"*

Here is a great example of leadership. Boaz has employed capable workers and has appointed a reliable foreman to supervise the work. Boaz comes to check on the work. He greets the workers cordially, with godly respect. He recognizes their hard and effective work. He trusts them.

They respond to him with a blessing from God. They respect Boaz. They are happy to see him come. They are eager to show him what they have accomplished. Boaz, the competent, confident, caring leader, has established a bond of loyalty and respect with his workers and their foreman.

Boaz then notices Ruth gleaning in the field. He enquires about her—respectfully—calling her a "young woman." There is no crudeness or harshness about Boaz. He is "an officer and a gentleman."

For women: Noble Character

> *Ruth 2:8-12, 3:11: "So Boaz said to Ruth, 'My daughter, listen to me. Don't go and glean in another field and don't go away from here. Stay here...' At this she [Ruth] bowed down with her face to the ground. She asked him [Boaz], 'Why have I found such favor in your eyes that you notice me, a foreigner?' Boaz replied, 'I have been told all about what you have done for your mother-in-law since the death of your husband... May the Lord repay you for what you have done. May you be richly rewarded by the Lord, the God of Israel, under whose wings you have come to take refuge... All the people of my town know that you are a woman of noble character.'"*

Ruth's unselfish service had earned her the highest accolade and best reputation any young woman could ever hope to achieve: to be known as a woman of "noble character."

For both men and women: God Honors Right Choices

> *Ruth 4:13: "So Boaz took Ruth and she became his wife... And the Lord enabled her to conceive, and she gave birth to a son"* (who was the grandfather of David, the king).

The marriage took place after an honorable and open courtship.

Ruth did it right. She chose service over husband-hunting. And eventually God rewarded her with a godly husband.

In 1 Corinthians 7, the Apostle Paul addresses the situation of young, unmarried women. Paraphrased and summarized, Paul says: Don't make husband-hunting the focus of your life. Instead, make the Lord's service the focus of your life. Find a ministry, a work which honors the Lord, which you can perform for your entire life, and devote yourself enthusiastically to that ministry. Give yourself fully to the cause of Christ, as a giving person, not a getting person. You will become known as a woman of "noble character." And then, in His own time and if He pleases, the Lord will give you a godly husband.

Trail Marker #26
Sexuality

Recently we had a lovely young woman, a deeply committed Christian, visit us for several days. We had many in-depth conversations with her. She had just graduated from a Christian college and was considering the next step in her life.

Before our friend departed, she and my wife had a long personal conversation. At the end, my wife asked her if she had any other deep concerns which she had not yet expressed. After a long pause, our friend brought up the subject of sexuality and her deep desire to be married and have children.

Since our friend gets our Trail Markers, they discussed the last part of Trail Marker #25: "Don't make husband-hunting the focus of your life. Instead, make the Lord's service the focus of your life... You will become known as a woman of 'noble character.' And then, in His own time and if He pleases, the Lord will give you a godly husband."

In almost every really deep conversation we have had with young people, both male and female, over the last few years, the subject eventually gets around to sexuality.

It is a freeing realization to know that it is GOD who created you as a sexual being. He "created them male and female." You are not "evil" because you have sexual feelings.

Read Song of Solomon 8:6b-7a:

> "...love [sexual desire] is as strong as death, its jealousy [ardor] as unyielding as the grave. It [sexual desire] burns like blazing fire, like a mighty flame. Many waters cannot quench love; rivers cannot sweep it away."

Sexual desire is a basic instinct, imbedded in every human being by God's design, both for the propagation of the race and for the fulfillment of happiness in marriage. Sexual desire is there in every person, and it cannot be extinguished or quenched or washed away.

But it is not to be aroused "before its time," which means marriage. Sexual arousal is to be confined within the boundaries of a secure, permanent, faithful marriage where frequent consummation is actually commanded. It is only in the freedom and security of marriage that the sexual relationship between a man and a woman can be experienced in its pure beauty, its unimaginable excitement, and its full and lasting satisfaction.

Now look at Genesis 6:2:

> *"The sons of God saw that the daughters of humans were beautiful, and they married...them."*

Men are naturally attracted to women. God made men that way. By the time a girl is in her mid-teens, she has become a lightning rod for men of all ages. Girls need to realize this and develop a strong "sales resistance" toward all men.

Also, girls do not need to decorate their faces or expose their bodies in order to attract men. Men are attracted to them by nature. Men, from their early teens throughout their whole lives, whether they are married or single, constantly experience this attraction. But men of character will keep their distance and save for marriage the consummation of this attraction.

A tip to girls regarding physical attraction in a dating relationship: In most situations, a boy will go as far as the girl will let him go. Girls, you must make boundary decisions in advance, lest in the heat of the moment you give away forever a precious part of yourself—a part of yourself which is absolutely necessary for your long-term mental and emotional health, a part of yourself which you can never get back.

Reaching Your Destination

A few years ago, we took four grandchildren to Jordan and Israel. After five wonderful days in Jordan, we crossed over the Jordan River by the Allenby Bridge into Israel.

On our third day in Israel, having spent the first two days exploring Jerusalem, we drove down to Masada, a flat-topped, treeless mountain of rock rising almost vertically 1,000 feet up from the desert floor on the west shore of the Dead Sea.

Masada is famous because, in 70 A.D., a large group of Jewish extremists called Zealots revolted against the Romans in Jerusalem. The revolt eventually failed, and a remnant of the rebels, numbering 960 men, women and children, retreated to the old fortress on top of Masada, where they held out for many months against a Roman siege.

When the Romans were on the verge of overtaking Masada, the Zealots committed mass suicide rather than surrender to the enemy. According to a contemporary historian, only two women and five children survived.

Today Masada is an Israeli national monument. You can ascend to the top either by cable car or by climbing up the 1,000-foot cliff on a steep, winding trail called the "Snake Trail."

Naturally, our grandchildren opted to climb up the ancient Snake Trail, which has existed for centuries. My wife chose the 10-minute cable car ride up. At age 83, and wanting to impress my grandchildren, I decided to attempt the climb up the Snake Trail as sort of a "last hurrah" to a long career of mountain climbing. A good friend, an Israeli, went with me to give me a hand in the event I gave out.

Our grandchildren made the 1,000-foot climb in 45 minutes.

It took me almost two hours.

The key to my success was starting out with a slow but steady pace, resting every 15 minutes or so, and keeping my eyes on the goal: the cable car station at the top of the cliff.

By walking at a slow, steady pace, I never got winded. By resting every 15 minutes or so, my legs never gave out. By looking up at the goal every few minutes, I could mark my progress. It encouraged me greatly to see the goal coming closer and closer, even though it seemed to be impossibly distant at the beginning.

After spending about an hour on the plateau at the top of Masada examining the ancient trenches, battlements and dwellings, we headed down. My wife and I, along with our three granddaughters, decided to take the cable car. Our 19-year-old grandson decided to run down the steep, rocky trail. It took him 17 minutes. He could hardly walk for the next four days, his legs were so sore.

In climbing the Christian mountain, it is keeping a steady pace, getting the necessary rest and keeping your eye on the goal that brings eventual "success."

The Bible speaks of steadiness, perseverance, courage, keeping your body under control, pressing on, keeping your shoulder to the plow, not turning back (or even looking back), and, most importantly, keeping your focus on your goal.

Let me paraphrase what the Apostle Paul states in Philippians:

> *I keep my body under control... I press on toward the mark of the high calling of God in Christ Jesus...[which is]...to know Him, and the power of His resurrection, and the fellowship of His suffering, being willing to be conformed unto His death.*

What IS that goal?

It is to become like Jesus—as Paul said, to be "conformed to the image of Jesus Christ."

The Christian life IS like climbing a mountain. It is not impossible. But it is hard. And many give up and go back down to a life of sin and sloth and degradation in the valley below.

However, there is true joy and fulfillment in continuing the climb, because we have a Companion who is always there beside us to strengthen us when we grow weary and to encourage us when we begin to doubt whether the climb is really worth the effort.

> *I have decided to follow Jesus,*
> *No turning back, no turning back.*
> —Old hymn

Trail Marker #28
When a Trail Marker Points in the Wrong Direction

We had just arrived by bus in Split, Croatia, on the northeastern coast of the Adriatic Sea, which lies between Italy on the west and Greece and the Balkans on the east.

We had been in Bulgaria for a teaching conference and had taken the train from Sofia, Bulgaria, to Belgrade, Serbia, where we spent the night. The next day we went, again by train, from Belgrade south into Montenegro and down to the capital of Podgorica, where we again spent the night.

Before dawn the next morning, we got a bus, which took us along the coast of Montenegro, across a tiny slice of Bosnia-Herzogovenia, to Dubrovnik in Croatia, often called "the jewel of the Adriatic." We spent a couple of fascinating hours in this ancient walled city on the coast of the Adriatic Sea.

Then, in mid-afternoon, we caught another bus, which went north along the fantastically beautiful Dalmatian coast of the Adriatic to Split, where Roman Emperor Diocletian had a magnificent vacation palace.

It was dark when we arrived and we were exhausted from the activities of a long but wonderful day. We had a reservation at a small hotel near the bus station, one of those typical European hotels where you enter from the sidewalk into a tiny registration office and then walk (or take a 3-foot-by-3-foot elevator) up to where there are three or four bedrooms on each floor, with one public bath on each floor.

We got ourselves oriented with a pocket compass before we ventured out of the bus station and into the night. We knew the street address of the hotel and had an Internet map showing the bus station, with an arrow pointing to the hotel about three blocks away. Pulling our suitcases, we walked out of the bus station into a light, chilly rain, expecting to be at our hotel in no more than five minutes.

But something seemed wrong. When we got to the right street, the street numbers seemed to run opposite to what our map indicated. Using a flashlight, we oriented the map with our compass. But the street numbers still appeared to be reversed.

We decided to disregard the street numbers and go where the arrow on the map indicated the hotel was located. But when we got to the point of the arrow, there was no hotel—only large, darkened office buildings.

Thinking that the arrow might be slightly off target, we went two long blocks further down the deserted, narrow, dimly lit street—but still no hotel, just gloomy, hostile-looking warehouses. So we stopped and prayed for wisdom.

It was now blowing as well as raining. Despite our umbrellas, we and our suitcases were getting wet.

We returned to the point of the arrow and decided to retrace our steps back toward the bus station and try again. More prayer.

This time we decided to follow the street numbers and locate the street address of the hotel. We walked for at least four blocks past the bus station before we found the street number of the hotel. But there was no hotel at that number. Again, more prayer.

We looked down several side streets and finally saw a dingy sign hanging above the sidewalk announcing our hotel. Our hearts leaped with joy. By this time, we had been on our search for about 45 minutes. Thank you, Lord!

We found the entrance under the sign and went in. It did not look like a hotel. There in the dimly lit, smoke-filled room was a long bar and a number of tables filled with men and women smoking, drinking and laughing. A few couples and some singles were dancing. The music was loud, heavy metal. We shouted at the bartender, asking where we could register. He spoke no English.

An older, rather disheveled man came up and asked, in very broken English, if he could help us. An angel? We told him the name of the hotel we were looking for and pointed to the sign above the entrance.

A moment went by while he looked us over. Then he laughed and said the hotel had moved several years before, but no one had bothered to take down the old sign. We weren't laughing.

He said the hotel was just around the corner, less than half a block away. We thanked him, and thanked God, and walked out. We easily found our hotel entrance a couple of minutes later under a neat, friendly, brightly lit sign. We walked in, soaked to the bone, and presented our passports to the desk clerk, a very friendly, courteous young man who spoke excellent English. We thanked God for caring for us.

What should have taken five minutes actually took more than an hour. Why? Because at least three of our important "trail markers" had been wrong: the arrow on the map, the street address of the hotel, and the hotel sign hanging over the entrance to the disco.

So what are the lessons?

First: Always be prepared for the occasional situation when the trail marker is wrong. Carry a compass, a flashlight, a map, and as much information about your destination as you can find. And carry a loud whistle in case you are assaulted.

Second: When you realize something is wrong with the directions, stop and pray for wisdom and protection.

Third: Think. Reassess. Consider the options. Make the best choice you can, depending on God for wisdom.

Fourth: Always take note of the route back to a known point (like the bus station).

And fifth: Don't panic or despair. God has promised never to leave us or forsake us.

Nothing made by man is perfect. So be prepared. Only the trail markers in God's Word can be relied on to be right—all the time.

> Isaiah 40:8: "The grass withers and the flowers fall, but the Word of our God endures forever."

Trail Marker #29
Decisions

Recently, an 11-year-old neighbor boy, accompanied by his mother, paid us a visit. His mother had called a couple of days earlier to ask if her son could interview me to fulfill a home school writing requirement.

His task was to interview an "older man" to identify some "lessons learned" that I had garnered during my lifetime.

Sammy is very bright. Both his mother and father are keen Christians. The tone of the interview indicated that Sammy might have had some help from his parents in developing his questions. No problem there—good parents.

After asking some brief warm-up biography questions ("Where were you born?" "What did you like to do when you were 11?" "Did you have brothers and sisters?") Sammy got right to the point.

"How has your faith in Jesus Christ affected your everyday actions?"

Good question. In fact, a GREAT question.

I was now up to bat. The pitch was a waist-high fastball. Could I knock it out of the park?

I thought, "I must be honest, be clear, be brief. Give him the truth. That's what he wants and deserves."

My answer: "Jesus has influenced every decision I have made since my decision to follow Him."

To live is to make decisions. Big ones. Small ones. Permanent ones. Temporary ones. Important ones. Minor ones.

The art of life is the art of decision-making.

Sammy was intrigued and took lots of notes.

Now for you men and women reading this, put yourselves in these situations:

Men and women: You wake up in the morning. First decision: Should I get up NOW and do my Bible reading? Or should I stay in bed for a few more minutes, since that movie last night kept me up later than usual and I need to be alert today? "Jesus, what *should* I do?"

What do you think His answer might be?

Women: Next decision: "Jesus, what should I wear to class (or work) this morning?" A bit more complicated.

Jesus' reply: "Anything in your closet appropriate for today's activities. But not that new green and yellow thing you wore last week. It exposes more of your body than I consider modest. It is not honoring to Me. Surely you must recall that several men were more 'friendly' than usual when you wore that dress. Wonder why? Were they admiring your intelligence, your godliness? And oh, like your Dad has told you several times, those torn, dirty jeans really do make you look cheap. Yuk! Not becoming for a girl of your quality and character."

Men: You are at work or changing class. "Uh-oh. Here comes Jerry. What a nerd. Should I try to avoid him? Oh, Lord, what should I do?"

Jesus' reply: "What are you? A man or a mouse? Be strong. Be a man. Look beyond your personal likes. Jerry is insecure. He feels inadequate. He doesn't have any friends. And He doesn't know Me. But he sees Me in you. He admires you. What should you do? Befriend him! That's what you should do. Show him some attention, some of MY love. Encourage him. Invite him to your church. Maybe I will work a miracle in his life—because of you."

Men: Leaving Walmart, you spot a really, *really* attractive young lady trying to get a large item into her small, late-model car. "Yes! Of course. I need to go over and give her a hand. An opportunity to help someone in need! She might hurt her back or something. Never can tell."

Just as you get near her car, you see another lady, this one a bit older, with two small children and a baby, struggling to get a big package into her not-so-late model van. Looking back toward the first young lady, you think, "Lord, I don't even need to ask You on this one. It's a slam-dunk. First come, first served. Or in this case, first noticed, first helped. Isn't that the right way? Can't get diverted, you know. And that first girl, well, wow! She really is cute. Must be a Christian. Always help the Christian sisters first. Right?"

Jesus' reply: "Wrong!"

The need to make decisions goes on and on—until the last nail is hammered into your coffin.

Psalm 119:24 states, "Your commands are my delight. They are my advisors."

Psalm 119:105 states: "Thy Word is a lamp unto my feet, a light unto my path."

Whatever the decision, ask Jesus, and He will give you something from His Word. That is, IF you are reading, studying, and memorizing His Word.

Psalm 119:11 states, "Thy Word have I hidden in my heart [memorized] that I might not sin against Thee [by making wrong decisions]."

So how has my faith in Jesus Christ affected my everyday actions?

Since I made the decision to follow Him as my Lord and Savior, Jesus has been involved in every decision I have made.

Trail Marker #30
My First Trail Marker

A trail marker is a signpost which points where the trail goes. The first trail marker is the most important.

The small Swiss alpine town of Lauterbrunnen is the starting point for several beautiful mountain trails. Each winds upward to a different destination. Each trail proceeds through pastures and woods, over streams, up steep slopes and past farm animals and picturesque cottages. On the way to its destination, each trail provides breathless views of tall, snow-capped mountains, sheer cliffs and awesome waterfalls.

So, take your pick!

But if you want to go to a particular destination, you must find the trail marker that identifies the trail leading to that destination.

My parents wanted me to follow Jesus, who is the Way, the Truth and the Life. They provided me with my first trail marker, pointing in the direction of God.

A few nights ago I knelt beside my bed to say my prayers (a practice my parents instilled in me). I was dog-tired and already almost asleep. I automatically started saying the first prayer I ever knew. I hadn't said it since I was a child. As I started to say it, I realized it was my first trail marker, the first signpost that eventually led me to faith in Jesus Christ as my Lord and Savior.

Could I remember it all? I started, and after a few hesitations and stumbles I was able to repeat it as I had memorized it at about age four—a long, long time ago:

Now I lay me down to sleep.
I pray Thee Lord my soul to keep.
If I should die before I wake,

I pray Thee Lord my soul to take.
I thank Thee for Thy tender care
And all that makes the world so fair.
Bless my loved ones each and all.
Guide my footsteps lest I fall.
Keep me through the coming day
In all I do and all I say.

"In Jesus' Name. Amen."

Simple, but profound. My first trail marker—at the beginning of the trail—which led me eventually to Jesus.

Trust but Verify

This morning I went to our local bank with a question. My monthly statement, which I received yesterday, did not show a sizeable deposit I had made a couple of weeks ago.

The teller, a long-time friend, quickly found the error. When she had made out the deposit slip, she had written the account number correctly. But the bank's computer scanner had read one digit incorrectly, and my deposit was sent to another account.

She called me a few minutes ago to state that the money had now been placed in my account. It was the first mistake the bank had made in my account in over 29 years.

I trust the bank, but I also read the monthly account statement carefully.

Many years ago I went to a military hospital for a routine checkup. It was a Friday morning. Late that afternoon, a doctor called to state that my blood work revealed an extremely high calcium level. I asked him what this might mean. He replied that it almost always indicated advanced thyroid cancer. He wanted to see me first thing Monday morning for further checks.

It was a difficult weekend as my wife and I discussed options before God in view of what might be my death within a few months.

When I went back to the hospital, the first thing they did was take another blood sample. An hour later the reading came back, and it was normal. Perplexed, the doctor made a quick check of the procedure followed the previous Friday. He found that one of the medics had switched my name with someone else—who DID truly have a high level of calcium in his blood.

After I retired from the Army, I worked as a part-time consultant for a multimillion-dollar computer systems firm in Washington, D.C. One day the chairman of the board announced that the company had been swindled out of $1.4 million. A few days earlier, the chief financial officer for the firm, a brilliant and trusted middle-aged single lady of high reputation, failed to show up for work. After a few phone calls, it was determined that her apartment was empty and she had flown to for Mexico City the night before. There the trail vanished.

That afternoon, an audit of the books by an outside firm revealed that $1.4 million was missing.

Apparently, shortly after she was hired two years before, the lady had discovered a flaw in the company's internal auditing system and had been able to redirect several thousand dollars a week from the company's income flow to her personal account, which she had emptied and closed before leaving for Mexico.

We live in a fallen world. Banks can make mistakes. Hospitals can make mistakes. And when presented with the opportunity, good people sometimes do evil things.

When President Reagan was dealing with the Soviet Union on nuclear arms control, his policy was to "trust, but verify."

The Scripture tells us that we should be as wise as serpents but as harmless as doves.

The Apostle Paul often prayed that his converts might have insight, wisdom and discernment.

Blind trust—in anything or anyone (but Jesus)—is NOT a Christian virtue. Trust? Yes. But in important matters, verify the statements and claims of others.

And pay close attention to your bank statement.

Trail Marker #32
In the Beginning (for Me)

Recently my wife and I traveled to my hometown on the Atlantic coast of Southeast Florida to visit extended family and see old high school friends. We saw scores of relatives, young and old. Most are Christians. It was a joyful time of fellowship in the Lord.

Not so with my high school friends. Although we had fun reminiscing, there was little spiritual content to our conversations. Only two or three of the 15 or so we saw are living in close communion with God.

In high school, most of us attended church and lived relatively good, moral lives. But I cannot recall any who knew Jesus Christ as Lord and Savior. My parents were solidly moral Midwesterners who had moved to Florida after World War I. I grew up in the Community Church because there was no Methodist Church (my father's background) or Christian Church (my mother's background). As I recall, there were five mainline churches in town: the Catholic Church, the Baptist Church, the Episcopal Church, the Lutheran Church and the Community Church.

The pastor of the Community Church was a wonderful old man who had moved to Florida when he retired from teaching theology at a Northern seminary. He was persuaded by several men in our small town (my father included) to start an inclusive, inter-denominational Protestant church, which the men named the "Community Church."

Our pastor preached beautiful sermons, primarily urging personal integrity and good works for society, frequently quoting great poets such as Longfellow, Keats, Shelley, Shakespeare, Wordsworth and so on. They were soothing, comforting sermons, emphasizing that everything works out for the best and that good will eventually triumph over evil. He often spoke of God, but I never heard anything about Jesus except for an occasional parable.

When I was a junior in high school, I started going to the Baptist Church because most of my athlete friends went there. The preacher did preach from the Bible and spoke about being saved, but I had absolutely no idea what he was talking about.

During the summer between my junior and senior years, I had a major "spiritual experience" which I never told anyone about. It left me in wrenching despair and utter confusion. I lost whatever faith I had and began to believe that life was totally meaningless.

So how did I and most of my extended family become believers?

I can take no credit for it. The credit belongs to some faithful Christian cadets at West Point who coerced me to attend a Bible study on Sunday afternoons, the only afternoon of the very regimented cadet week when I could goof off, vegetate and sack out. This was during my second year.

During those Sunday afternoon Bible studies, God began to speak to my heart through His Word. The Bible states that "faith comes by hearing" [reading, studying, reflecting on] the Truth in the Word of God. This was my experience. Over a period of several months, I fully embraced the gospel message that I found in the Word of God and, by faith, opened the door of my heart for Jesus to enter in. In particular, it was reading and thinking on the claims of Jesus in the Gospel of John (the great "I AMs") that made the difference.

Paul states in II Corinthians 5:17, "If any man be in Christ, he is a new creature. Old things have passed away. Behold, all things are become new."

This was abundantly true for me. The old wrenching despair and spiritual confusion were replaced by faith, assurance, confidence, hope, joy and purpose for living. I was a new man.

During graduation week at West Point, our small band of Christian brothers held a picnic at Delafield Pond honoring our parents and families. We sang hymns. Cadets gave testimonies. A young minister explained the gospel. My parents, then in their fifties, listened carefully and were impressed. My siblings met and mingled with Christian cadets. During the following year, both of my parents put their trust and faith in Jesus Christ. So also did three of my four siblings. And during the decades to come, they all married

Christians and raised their many children in the nurture and admonition of the Lord.

Want to change your personal world for generations to come?

Get your friends and family members into the Word of God.

> *"Faith comes by hearing [reading, studying, reflecting on] the Truth in the Word of God" (Romans 10:17).*

> *"The Word of God is living and powerful, sharper than a double-edged sword, piercing even to the dividing asunder of soul and spirit, and of the joints and marrow, and is a discerner of the thoughts and attitudes of the heart" (Hebrews 4:12).*

Trail Marker #33
The Crunch Point

In the last Trail Marker I wrote: "During the summer between my junior and senior years, I had a major 'spiritual experience' which I never told anyone about at the time. It left me in wrenching despair and utter confusion. I lost whatever faith I had and began to believe that life was totally meaningless."

Briefly, here is what happened.

Until the summer of my 17th birthday, I had always had the vague impression that the whole world revolved around me. I was the center of everything. High school was great. I had many friends. During my junior year, the Vero Beach Indians won the Florida State basketball championship with me playing center, and I was the new team captain. We did well in football, and I was a unanimous choice for All-Conference. I was elected president of the senior class. I had some musical talent and played trumpet in the school band and piano in a student dance band. I reveled in the affirmation of both students and faculty.

Then it happened.

It was wartime, and I had volunteered for the graveyard shift (midnight until 6:00 AM) three times a week on a civil defense spotter tower on the beach. The purpose of these spotter towers, which had been constructed every 15 miles or so all the way from Jacksonville down to Miami, was to detect aircraft activity out over the ocean and report it by telephone back to Central Control in Orlando. The towers were about 40 feet high and had a cabin on the top, open except for a roof. I worked in blackout, except for a small flashlight with a red filter over the lens.

Alone in the dark, with only three or four aircraft to report each night (estimated altitude, direction of flight, number of engines), it was lonely and boring. And I was an action person.

I started trying to stay awake and keep my mind busy by observing the planets and stars. I got hold of a publication called "The Monthly Evening

Star Map." I found charts of all the stars and constellations observable in the eastern sky of the Northern Hemisphere. It was arranged by month and showed when various constellations and first magnitude stars would rise above the horizon in the eastern sky between midnight and dawn.

It was a fascinating study. Pretty soon I could identify all of the major constellations and first magnitude stars in the summer sky during the hours between midnight and 6:00 AM.

(To this day, the summer sky in the Northern Hemisphere, after midnight, looks familiar and friendly, although I'm not up at that time very often to enjoy it.)

All well, so far.

But then things began to change. I began to think deeply—for the first time in my life. The questions came slowly but powerfully. How far away are the stars? How long have the stars been there? What is behind the stars? Where is the end of space? When was the beginning of time? Will time ever end? Bottom line question: Is there a limit to space, to time?

My mind couldn't cope with limitless time and limitless space. Like a basketball game or football game, there HAD to be a starting whistle and an ending whistle. And like a basketball court or a football field, everything HAD to have boundaries.

And then, the killer questions began to emerge. Who am I? Really, who am I? I know my name, age, sex, family, friends. But how did this consciousness, this awareness, this comprehension, this "life" which is the *essential me*, come to be lodged in this specific body, and at this time, and in this place? Why wasn't this *essential me* lodged in a girl's body, a century ago, in Africa, of another family, of another race? And what would happen when my body died? Would the *essential me* also die? Would I simply become a stinking, rotting, worm-eaten corpse, like some dead animal, with no awareness of anything? Total oblivion?

I had no answers, and I began to get frightened. I had grown up in Sunday school and church and knew a lot of hymns and Bible stories. But David and Goliath and the Good Samaritan were not relevant in this situation.

They provided no answers to the searching questions which were searing my soul.

At the end of the summer, approaching what I had thought earlier would be a triumphant senior year, I was in despair, lost in the woods, floundering in a mass of intellectual quicksand, believing that life had no essential meaning and that oblivion was the destiny of all human flesh.

To make a long story short, I made it through senior year and, a month after graduation, entered West Point as a plebe.

The old undergirding self-confidence, which had stood me in good stead until that fateful summer a year before, was totally gone. Below the surface was despair, confusion, fear. I was simply faking it in my daily life, going through the motions, trying not to even think of "reality" as I then conceived it; believing that, no matter what I might do, I would eventually end up—like everyone else—as rotting roadkill.

Then, a year and a half into West Point, another powerful "spiritual experience" took place, which totally changed my life. I came face to face with Jesus Christ. How did this happen?

Stay tuned for the next Trail Marker.

Dawn

Trail Marker #33 ended as follows: "Then, a year and a half into West Point, another powerful spiritual experience took place, which totally changed my life. I came face to face with Jesus Christ. How did this happen?"

Life at West Point was tough and regimented. Cadets lived outwardly disciplined lives, worked hard at academics and sports, carefully followed the Cadet Honor Code ("A cadet will not lie, cheat or steal, or tolerate those who do"), took seriously their commitment to the Academy, the Army and the Nation, and looked inspiring and sinless at weekend full-dress parades.

But underneath, it was different.

On weekends, college girls flooded the Academy grounds, and cadet conversation at the end of a weekend was often laced with extremely graphic descriptions of sexual exploits. Although cadets were not allowed to drink alcoholic beverages on the Academy grounds or within 30 miles thereof, on weekends away in New York City or on summer training trips around the country, heavy drinking and drunkenness among cadets was not uncommon.

I was now away from my family, my high school friends and my small hometown. I felt myself being pulled away from my moral roots. Quite sincerely, I did not want this to happen. In high school, staying clean sexually and not drinking had been a matter of personal pride. I knew that if I did yield, I would lose something which was part of the *essential me*.

But the temptation was strong and persistent. Knowing my desire to stay sexually clean, my roommate once regaled me with descriptions of his girlfriend undressing before him (from fully clothed until totally naked). And drinking a Coke or a ginger ale at a cadet beer bust on a summer trip was not the best way to gain the acceptance of my peers, which I greatly desired.

I knew I was fraying at the edges, and I knew I had to find some solid purpose for resisting these temptations—some source of strength to maintain a life of moral integrity.

Through a cadet organization, I had come into contact with some cadets who seemed different. They were good cadets, good students, friendly, confident, and their language was clean—very different from that of the average cadet. About the middle of my sophomore year, one of these cadets invited me to attend a morning devotional group that met daily for a few minutes between breakfast and our first class. He said that, among other things, they sang hymns.

I loved music and had always enjoyed singing hymns in Sunday school and church. So I started going. It was fun, and I met a number of other cadets who seemed genuinely interested in living morally clean lives. The only thing I couldn't understand was when, each morning, one of these cadets would stand up, quote some Bible verses I had never heard before and then talk briefly about his personal relationship with Jesus Christ. I was clueless!

One day some of these cadets invited me to attend a Sunday afternoon Bible study. This seemed absurd. Sunday afternoon was the only time of the week I could call my own. We had classes until noon Saturday. Saturday afternoon, there was always some sports event to attend. Saturday evening, there was frequently a cadet *hop* (dance) where you might be able to make friends with a *femme* (a college girl up at West Point for the weekend). Then, Sunday morning after breakfast, we formed up in full-dress gray and marched up the hill to attend the formal, mandatory chapel service.

Sunday afternoon certainly was not a time I wanted to attend a Bible study.

But they persisted, and they were cadets who seemed to have the moral foundation and internal strength I was seeking, who lived above the common level of cadet life. So I started going.

The Bible states, "Faith comes by hearing, and hearing by the Word of God" (Romans 10:17).

I started into this Bible study experience without any faith at all. It was a result of this Bible study that I came to faith in Jesus Christ. When I graduated from West Point over two years later, I went out into the Army as a believer in Jesus Christ, fully committed to follow Him and live for Him to the fullest extent possible.

In the next Trail Marker, I will describe the internal, intellectual process by which this Bible study transformed me from a skeptical nonbeliever into an enthusiastic believer.

Trail Marker #35
From Darkness to Light

The last Trail Marker ended with these words: "I started into this Bible study experience without any faith at all. It was a result of this Bible study that I came to faith in Jesus Christ. When I graduated from West Point over two years later, I went out into the Army as a believer in Jesus Christ, fully committed to follow Him and live for Him to the fullest extent possible."

Here is the process by which this Bible study transformed me from a skeptical nonbeliever into an enthusiastic believer.

I don't even remember what we were studying. We were in the New Testament. That is all I remember. But the words I was hearing were powerful. Even though I had earlier relegated the Bible into the category of ancient history, these words began to strike home. They seemed to be alive, to have current relevance—and most important of all, they were speaking to me.

This Jesus I was hearing about was completely new to me. He was saying words which were truly penetrating my soul. He was speaking about life on earth as though it was important and had meaning and purpose. He spoke about life after death, of an eternal home in heaven. He spoke about HIS sacrifice on the cross for MY sins so that I could have this eternal heritage. He said He loved me and really cared for me.

Slowly, I began to believe what I was hearing, to trust Him, to believe Him, to follow Him.

And as I began to believe, my life began to change. The old despair was replaced by hope, darkness by light, confusion by joy, the wrenching stench of death by the sweet fragrance of life. It was a whole new realization that life had meaning and purpose, and that by trusting in Jesus, there would be a happy ending. The dark fog of doubt and despair was being dissipated by a beautiful sunrise of faith and hope. I felt like I had been reborn into a new and different life.

This did not take place in an instant. Coming to faith in Christ really WAS like the sunrise. Gradually the darkness of night was penetrated by the first rays of dawn, and then the sun appeared on the horizon, and slowly it rose up until it was high in the sky, and light and hope and joy and peace and love and purpose came into my world and gave light to my life.

This sun—this confidence in God the Father, God the Son, God the Holy Spirit—has stayed high in my sky for over 70 years. Of course, there have been clouds, and rain, and darkness and some severe storms. But always I have known that the sun was still there, and that eventually light would break through the darkness and once again flood my soul with His grace and love and peace.

Is there darkness in your life and soul? Then go to the Word of God. Believe it. Believe Jesus. For He has said, "I am the light of the world. He that cometh to Me shall not walk in darkness but shall have the light of life" (John 8:12).

> "For the Word of God is living and powerful, sharper than any double-edged sword, piercing even unto the dividing asunder of soul and spirit, and the joints and marrow, and is a discerner of the thoughts and intents of the heart" (Hebrews 4:12).

Trail Marker #36
The Word of God and the Christian Mind

Psalm 1:1-2: "Blessed is the man…whose delight is in the law of the Lord; and on His law he meditates day and night."

"You can never have a Christian mind without reading the Scriptures regularly, because you cannot be deeply influenced by that which you do not know. If you are filled with God's Word, your life can then be informed and directed by God— your domestic relationships, your child-rearing, your career, your ethical decisions, your interior morality. The only way to a Christian mind is through God's Word!"
—the late Lieutenant General William K. Harrison, USA, president of the Officers' Christian Fellowship for 17 years

Psalms 119:24: "Your words are my delight. They are my advisors."

Trail Marker #37
Sixty Years on the Marriage Trail

The year 2012 was our 60th anniversary year. Instead of trying to have a family reunion, gathering together four children and their spouses, 21 grandchildren and 17 great-grandchildren, we decided to visit each one of them sometime during the year.

We went to Alaska, Texas, Ohio and Italy. We did miss a couple of Alaskan great-grandchildren, who were born after our trip there.

In November 2012, we took two of our grandchildren who lived in Italy, ages 12 and 10, on a trip to Norway, Sweden and Finland. We flew from Venice, Italy, to Oslo, Norway, took a train to Stockholm, Sweden, and then a ferry (the size of a large cruise ship) to Helsinki, Finland. We flew back to Venice from Helsinki via Riga, Latvia.

En route we stayed in the homes of friends, at small hotels and at youth hostels; ate fantastic Norwegian, Swedish and Finnish food; visited many museums, ancient churches and historic towns; and enjoyed the majestic Scandinavian scenery.

At 85 and 83, we couldn't move as fast or carry as much baggage as we used to. But the two children, themselves experienced travelers, were very helpful to their *Opa* and *Oma* (the German words for Grandfather and Grandmother) and provided us a great incentive to "keep on keeping on."

We have now taken 18 of our 21 grandchildren on trips to Europe or Israel and Jordan.

God has blessed us with a wonderful family. As we near the end of our own trail, we want to invest in our children, our grandchildren and our great-grandchildren with as much of our time and resources as we can. They are our legacy.

More than anything else, we want them to enjoy the rich and joyful life in Jesus that we have been privileged to enjoy.

In a real sense, we are THEIR TRAIL MARKERS along the Christian trail which leads to everlasting life in heaven with our triune God, the creator and sustainer of all life, both temporal and eternal—God the Father, God the Son and God the Holy Spirit.

Trail Marker #38
The Trail Heads Northwest to Alaska

Here is a "press release" from a few years back:

This coming Sunday afternoon (9 June) we leave on a 12-day trek by automobile to Alaska. The reason is a bit complex, but in a nutshell, we are driving our grandson's second car to Anchorage, loaded with wedding presents.

He is Second Lieutenant Chris Buckingham, Andy's middle son, recently commissioned in the Army through ROTC from the University of Virginia, and much more recently (last Saturday) married to a longtime friend from here in Pennsylvania, Sarah Bryan.

Chris recently moved to Ft. Richardson, Alaska, with the Army. He flew down here last Thursday for the wedding festivities. He and his bride, Sarah, are on their honeymoon right now and will fly to Alaska at week's end.

Chris's car is back in Alaska. Sarah has a well-used Infiniti SUV. This is the car that needs to get to Alaska, along with sundry wedding presents.

So Clara and I volunteered to drive it up. Of course, we have another son who lives about 40 miles north of Anchorage, in Palmer. This is our son Jim, plus wife Martha, and numerous children. So Clara and I will deliver the car and wedding presents to Chris and Sarah on about 22 June and then spend a week with Jim and family before returning home on 1 July by air.

En route to Alaska, we will stop to see our daughter Rebecca and her husband, Curt, in Ohio; visit with a foster grandson in Salt Lake City; spend a couple of days in the Olympic Mountains (Washington State) with retired longtime Army friends, Chaplain Jim and Robbie Edgren; and then drive on up through western Canada to Alaska.

Clara and I look forward to many hours of uninterrupted time together reading God's Word; praying; listening to audio books, teaching tapes and good music; and just enjoying the precious company of each other.

Stay tuned for the exciting sequel.

Trail Marker #39
Alaska or Bust

"What in the world were you thinking about, you old goat?" I asked the wrinkled, stoop-shouldered, white-haired old man staring at me in the mirror.

The 1999 Infinity SUV, loaded with wedding presents, was all gassed up and parked in our garage. We were leaving that day on a 6,500-mile driving trip from Bedford, Pennsylvania, to Ft. Richardson, Alaska. Ahead of us, through 13 states and two Canadian provinces, lay two major mountain ranges; several large cities (Indianapolis, St. Louis, Kansas City, Salt Lake City, Seattle); the seemingly endless plains of the Midwest; the vast emptiness of western Canada; stretches of road where it is 75 miles between gas stations; and the shifting, undulating road surfaces in northwest Canada and eastern Alaska caused by the freezing and thawing of the soggy terrain.

"What if the SUV breaks down? What if we have a flat tire? What if we have an accident? What if one of us gets sick? What if we can't find a motel? What if we are attacked by a bear? What if we are mugged? What if someone breaks into the SUV and steals the wedding presents?"

I finished shaving and turned away from the mirror, lest the image of that old geezer trying to change a tire in the Canadian wilderness frighten me so badly that I might decide to call it all off and go back to my comfy easy chair in front of the TV, watching the news.

Our grandson, an army lieutenant stationed at Ft. Richardson, Alaska, had recently flown home to get married. His bride had earlier been given the old SUV as a college graduation present from her parents. Our grandson's own car was up in Alaska. He could only get a few days leave for the wedding—not nearly enough time for a 10-day drive back to Alaska in his bride's SUV with her.

So my wife and I, at ages 84 and 86, had volunteered to drive the SUV, plus most of their wedding gifts, to Alaska for them. We had prayed it through time and again and prepared as well as we could.

Now it was time to fish or cut bait.

Away from the terrifying image in the mirror, I took consolation in remembering that Joshua was well over 80 years old when he invaded the Promised Land and fought the battle of Jericho. I prayed the prayer of Moses as he left Egypt: "Lord, if you don't go with us, we just can't go."

A voice whispered in my ear, saying, "Jesus said, 'I will never leave you or forsake you.'"

In World War II, General George Patton once told his division commanders, "Never take counsel of your fears."

So we backed out of the garage and headed west.

It could not have been a more enjoyable trip. En route we:

- Had no problem with the SUV.

- Experienced no illnesses.

- Had no accidents.

- Had no problem finding motels and gas stations.

- Were not attacked by bears or mugged.

- Did not have anything stolen.

- Burned 270 gallons of gasoline at 20 MPG at an average of about $4.00 per gallon (it was between $5.50 and $6.50 per gallon in Canada).

- Saw many bison, bear and wild sheep, one fox and one raccoon.

- Saw many spectacular snow-capped mountains, lakes, valleys, rivers, glaciers, forests (pine, spruce, fir, hemlock, cottonwood, birch), wheat fields, grain elevators, oil wells, freight trains, pickup trucks and RVs.

- Consumed many cinnamon buns (a favorite along the Alaska Highway).

- Successfully maneuvered the "turbulence" of the Alaska Highway in western Canada and eastern Alaska.

- Read eight books of the New Testament and listened to one John Grisham audio book, several CDs on ancient history, two John Stott CDs plus five or six classical and Christian music CDs.

- Spent many, many hours in prayer.

- And thoroughly enjoyed the uninterrupted time with each other.

When Jesus says, "I will never leave you or forsake you," He means it.

Trail Marker #40
Conclusion

We recently visited Israel with three grandchildren, ages 11, 12 and 13.

At 90 and 88, we couldn't move as fast or carry as much as we used to. But the three children, all experienced travelers, were very helpful to their *Opa* and *Oma*. Our slogan was: "We can all make it if we hold on to each other."

In one sense, Israel is just one big archeological dig.

And every dig unearths "trail markers."

It is so encouraging to find out that every major dig in the last several decades has confirmed biblical accounts. Recently, the ancient city of Gezer was discovered, buried deep under several layers of more recent cities. It was located exactly where the Bible places it.

The trail of the children of Israel from Egypt to the Promised Land is well-marked. Joshua left many trail markers (piles of stone), some of which are still standing, as he crossed the Jordan River, fought the battle of Jericho and went throughout the Promised Land, securing the whole area for God's people, the Israelites.

The whole Bible is a compendium of trail markers, showing us the way to authentic faith and purposeful, joyful Christian living.

As a married couple, we have been following the biblical trail markers for 65 years. It has been an amazing and adventurous journey. We have been blessed beyond measure.

Years ago, before we even knew each other, we each had decided to "follow Jesus, no turning back." Then, at our wedding, we each declared our commitment to each other—to love, enjoy and serve each other for all of our lives, no turning back.

God has blessed that commitment beyond our wildest dreams.

And we have hope for the future.

In the hymn, "Great is Thy Faithfulness," we sing that God gives us "strength for today and bright hope for tomorrow."

> *"May the God of hope fill YOU with all joy and peace as YOU trust in Him, so that YOU may overflow with hope, by the power of the Holy Spirit" (Romans 15:13).*

Made in the USA
Monee, IL
13 May 2024

58112184R00068